Chapters

Chapter 1
Introduction

We are passionate about educating people about money, this guide has been put together to give you a guide to what you need to know.

At Hartey Wealth Management Limited we provide clear independent financial advice and active investment management to businesses and personal clients We provide impartial, unbiased financial advice, with a view to protecting and enhancing our clients' wealth.

Having over a quarter of a century of experience in advising clients with all types of needs, we have helped and guided 1000's of people through the process of saving and retiring.

Our qualified advisers cover the whole financial services market. Whether you are seeking to build an investment portfolio or create a tax-efficient retirement strategy, we have the expertise to provide the answer. We base our business on clear goals and strong leadership. We deliver advice in a professional manner, always with our clients' best interests at heart.

Our Work is:

To help retirees and successful business people understand the risks they are taking and to help them realign this with the risk they are willing to take and to protect their downside.

1. The Financial Industry tells everyone to stay in the market in a downturn, when the professional money has already left the building. The conventional wisdom of blindly staying in the market does not take into account

your individual time horizon or the fact that the things that have failed are not necessarily the things that will do well moving forward.

2. Your Personal Time Horizon and your exit strategy are more important than stock selection.

3. We know that clients who move from risk to safety are much happier and confident about their future. Feeling trapped in underperforming assets just serves the industry and does not serve you or your peace of mind.

4. People are at their wealthiest at retirement and so your whole life's work is at risk. A profit is not a profit until it is taken. Realignment and rebalancing is a vital part of our investment approach.

5. The categorisation of your attitude to risk may be wrong. The Financial Industry likes to put you in a box. In reality, your attitude to risk will change on a regular basis, dependent on your employment, your earnings, the wider economy and your time horizon.

6. Our Relationship Based Approach can solve these issues, providing you financial peace of mind.

The following pages are detailed, but hopefully keeping it simple to guide you through the maze of financial products.

Chapter 2
Wealth goals why save

Reaching wealth goals and achieving personal ambitions are major objectives of the financial planning process. In order to make plans for the future you need to know where you are today and where you want to be in the future.

Wealth goal setting is very much like creating a business plan. You need to know a starting point and ending point, the time frame for 'exiting' (or reaching your goals), and the estimated cost involved.

Types of wealth goals

The three most common types are:

- Retirement planning or property purchase over the very long term (15 years or more)
- Life events, such as school fees over the medium term (10-15 years)
- Rainy day or lifestyle funds to finance goals such as a dream sports car over the medium to shorter term (5-10 years)

Wealth goals that really matter most.

It's important to consider and plan for which wealth goals really matter most. Instead, many people muddle through their financial lives, spending to meet the day-to- day expenses that dominate their attention. That's why to get what you want most, you must decide which wealth goals will take priority and work toward the lesser goals only after the really important ones are well provided for.

Approach to achieving your goals.

The minimum time horizon for all types of investing should be at least five years.

Whatever your personal wealth goals may be it is important to consider the time horizon at the outset, as this will affect your approach to achieving your goals. It also makes sense to revisit your goals at regular intervals to account for any changes to your personal circumstances, for example, the arrival of a new member to the family, or as you enter retirement.

Clearly define your specific goals

As a starting point, consider the goals you set previously and reflect on what worked and what didn't and why. Once you've done this, it's time to clearly define your specific goals. Most people tend to set wealth goals that are more about money than about things that motivate them emotionally.

SMART goals you truly value

Goals that are tied to what you truly value are often easier to achieve than goals that are simply tied to money. Part of what gives this goal its power is that it's SMART: **it is Specific, Measurable, Attainable, and Relevant and has a Timeline.**

Define your goal clearly

A wealth goal is the first step that sets you on a path and should be:

- **Specific** – 'To get wealthier' is not a specific or clear goal, but 'to achieve two thirds of your previous working lifetime income at 55 when you retire' is. The earliest you can retire from a defined contribution scheme (i.e. personal pension) is age 55 (rising to 57 in 2028)

- **Measurable** – Set deadlines for your wealth goals, such as the age at which you want to retire, or the timeline for buying a holiday home
- **Achievable** – Use your own income (and expected income) to set your wealth goals for the future. Don't count on inheriting money
    - **Relevant** – Create a personal financial bucket list of wealth goals, but always view it as a flexible document that will change with time as your interests and life situation changes
    - **Timeline** – Identify your time frame by categorising your objectives by short-term, medium- term and long-term wealth goals to provide focus and to help match your goals with appropriate savings and investments

A financial to do list provides important action steps that can help you keep your financial plans on track. Some of these include:

- Giving your portfolio a regular check-up to make sure your mix of investments accurately reflects your current goals, time frame, attitude to risk, tolerance of risk and capacity for risk/loss
- Taking full advantage of your employer's pension plan (if you're not doing this already)
- Tracking your spending to see where your money is going
- Calculating your net worth so that you understand where you stand financially
- Creating a legacy for future generations and/or charitable organisations that reflect your values

As crucial as a financial to do list is to your long-term financial security, creating a not-to-do list is equally important. That's because a not-to-do list can help you avoid some of the mistakes that may be keeping you from making the most of your money. For example, do not:

- Try to time the market. No one knows for certain which way the market will head next, instead be strategic and thoughtful about your investment decisions
- Make investing decisions in isolation. Rather, consider how each may impact your overall wealth goals
- Delay saving for retirement. The sooner you get started the greater the impact time and compounding may have on your ability to build financial security for the future
- Gain access to your retirement savings unless in an emergency. Taking money from your pension pot is like borrowing from your future to pay for your present needs
- Ignore the important role risk plays in your portfolio's ability to grow over time
- Minimise the impact of inflation on your money's future buying power
- Ignore your investments. Review your investments periodically to make sure they're performing as expected. If they're not, be ready to make changes as needed

Changing personal and financial situation.

Over time, your personal and financial situation is likely to change. Consider how this may affect your wealth goals, attitude to risk, tolerance of risk, capacity for risk/ loss and time frame, as well as your investment and protection planning requirements.

Make sure you have a properly drafted and signed Will. Check to see that your Will (and any trust) accurately reflects your wishes and that the beneficiaries on your pension plans and life insurance policies are up to date.

Chapter 3
Protection for you and your family

What would happen to you and your family in the event of unforeseen circumstances such as you losing your job, having a serious illness or dying prematurely? It's essential to make sure that you have adequate protection in place for you, your family and any dependants.

Everyone's protection requirements will differ and there's not a 'one size fits all' solution. If life takes a turn for the worse due to an accident, illness, or even death, it could mean financial hardship for you and anyone dependent on you.

Planning your legacy and passing on your wealth is another area that requires early planning. Benjamin Franklin was right when he said the only two certainties in life were 'death and taxes'. In addition, when it comes to Inheritance Tax, the two things collide. However, why should HM Revenue & Customs take some of your assets when you die – especially since you have probably already paid income tax on the money earned to buy them and capital gains tax on any profits.

To discuss your requirements or for further information, please contact us – we look forward to hearing from you.

Safeguarding your family's lifestyle

We all want to safeguard our family's lifestyle in case the worst should happen. But only a quarter (24%) of adults in the UK with children under 16 have any form of financial protection, a significant drop from 31% in 2013, according to research from the Scottish Widows Protection Report. With over half (54%) of this group admitting that their savings would last just a couple of months if they were unable to work, a significant protection gap exists for families in the UK.

Real Challenges for households

Almost half of households (46%) with children under 16 are now also reliant on two incomes, and a further 14% of this group state that parents or grandparents are dependent on their income. There would be real challenges for these households if one income were lost.

Replicating the modern family

While some government support is available in times of need, the current state bereavement benefits and support system is based on marriage or registered civil partnerships and doesn't yet replicate the modern family we see today. Unmarried couples and long-term partners are left in a welfare grey area – particularly when it comes to looking after their dependent children following the death of a parent.

People are realistic about the support available, with only 1% of those with children under 16 believing the state would look after their family if something were to happen to them. 45% of this group also believe that individuals should take personal responsibility for protecting their income through insuring against the unexpected happening to themselves or a loved one.

Source data: [1] Family and Childcare Trust – Childcare Costs Survey

Making the right decisions

With so many different protection options available making the right decision to protect your personal and financial situation can seem overwhelming.

There is a plethora of protection solutions that could help ensure that a lump sum or a replacement income becomes available to you in the event that it is needed. We can make sure that you are able to make the right decisions to deliver peace of mind for you and your family in the event of death, if you are too ill to work or if you are diagnosed with a critical illness.

You can choose protection-only insurance, which is called 'term insurance'. In its simplest form, it pays out a specified amount if you die within a selected period of years. If you survive, it pays out nothing. It is one of the cheapest ways overall of buying the cover you may need. Alternatively, a whole-of-life policy provides cover for as long as you live.

Life Assurance Options

* Whole-of-life assurance plans can be used to ensure that a guaranteed lump sum is paid to your estate in the event of your premature death. To avoid Inheritance Tax and probate delays, policies should be set up under an appropriate trust.
* Level term plans provide a lump sum for your beneficiaries in the event of your death over a specified term.
* Family income benefit plans give a replacement income for beneficiaries on your premature death.
* Decreasing term protection plans pay out a lump sum in the event of your death to cover a reducing liability for a fixed period, such as a repayment mortgage.

Simply having life assurance may not be sufficient. For instance, if you contracted a near-fatal disease or illness, how would you cope financially? You may not be able to work and so lose your income, but you are still alive so your life assurance does not pay out.

Income Protection Insurance (IPI), formerly known as 'permanent health insurance', would make up a percentage of your lost income caused by an illness, accident or disability.

Rates vary according to the dangers associated with your occupation, age, state of health and gender but IPI is particularly important if you are self-employed or if you do not have an employer that would continue to pay your salary if you were unable to work.

If you are diagnosed with suffering from one of a number of specified 'critical' illnesses, a critical illness insurance policy would pay out a tax-free lump sum if the event occurred during the term of your policy. Many life insurance companies offer policies that cover you for both death and critical illness.

Critical illness protection

The diagnosis of a serious illness can mean a very difficult time for your health and your wealth. However, critical illness cover can provide vital financial security when you need it most. Most homebuyers purchase life assurance when they arrange a mortgage but some overlook critical illness cover, another form of financial protection, that we are statistically more likely to need before reaching retirement.

The right peace of mind

You really need to find the right peace of mind when faced with the difficulty of dealing with a critical illness. Critical illness assurance pays a tax-free lump sum on diagnosis of any one of a list of specified serious illnesses, including cancer and heart attacks. The good news is that medical advances mean more people than ever are surviving life- threatening conditions that might have killed earlier generations. Critical illness cover can provide cash to allow you to pursue a less stressful lifestyle while you recover from illness, or use it for any other purpose.

It's almost impossible to predict certain events that may occur within our lives, so taking out critical illness cover for you and your family, or if you run a business or company, offers protection when you may need it more than anything else.

Exclusions and limitations

The illnesses covered are specified in the policy along with any exclusions and limitations which may differ between insurers. Critical illness policies usually only pay out once, so are not a replacement for income. Some policies offer combined life and critical illness cover. These pay out if you are diagnosed with a critical illness, or you die, whichever happens first.

If you already have an existing critical illness policy you might find that by replacing a policy you would lose some of the benefits if you have developed any illnesses since you took out the first policy. It is important to seek professional financial advice before considering replacing or switching your policy as pre-existing conditions may not be covered under a new policy.

Core specified conditions

All policies should cover seven core specified conditions. These are cancer, coronary artery bypass, heart attack, kidney failure, major organ transplant, multiple sclerosis and stroke. They will also pay out if a policyholder becomes permanently disabled because of injury or illness.

However, not all conditions are necessarily covered. The Association of British Insurers (ABI) introduced a set of best practice guidelines.

In May 2003, the ABI introduced other measures. These included conditions such as non-invasive skin cancers and less advanced cases of prostate cancer. Tumours that have not yet invaded the organ or tissue, and lymphoma or Kaposi's sarcoma in the presence of HIV are excluded.

There are also more restrictive conditions for heart attacks. There has to be evidence of typical chest pain or changes in the electrocardiogram (ECG), for example if a claim is to be successful. Cardiac conditions such as angina will not be covered.

Lifestyle changes

Some policies may allow you to increase your cover particularly after lifestyle changes such as marriage, moving home or having children. If you cannot increase the cover under your existing policy you could consider taking out a new policy just to 'top up' your existing cover.

A policy will provide cover only for conditions defined in the policy document. For a condition to be covered, your condition must meet the policy definition exactly. This can mean that some conditions, such as some forms of cancer, won't be covered if deemed insufficiently severe.

Similarly, some conditions may not be covered if you suffer from them after reaching a certain age, for example, many policies will not cover Alzheimer's disease if diagnosed after the age of 60.

Survival period

Very few policies will pay out as soon as you receive diagnosis of any of the conditions listed in the policy and most pay out only after a 'survival period'. This means that if you die within the specified number of days of meeting the definition of the critical illness given in the policy, the cover would not pay out.

How much you pay for critical illness cover will depend on a range of factors. These include; the type of policy you have chosen, your age, the amount you want the policy to pay out and whether or not you smoke.

Permanent total disability is usually included in the policy. Some insurers define 'permanent total disability' as being unable to work as you normally would as a result of sickness, while others see it as being unable to independently perform three or more 'Activities of Daily Living' as a result of sickness or accident.

Getting it covered

If you are single with no dependants critical illness cover can be used to pay off your mortgage, which means that you would have fewer bills or a lump sum to use if you became very unwell. In addition, if you are part of a couple it can provide much-needed financial support at a time of emotional stress.

While life assurance is often the priority of those with dependant family members, critical illness cover can be vital if you are the sole breadwinner, rely heavily on your income or are single. It provides a welcome financial boost at a time of emotional stress and financial hardship.

Before you take out critical illness cover you should obtain professional financial advice to make sure that it is right for you and offers sufficient cover.

Income protection insurance

Protecting your income is essential given the limited government support available. How would you pay the bills if you were sick or injured and couldn't work? Income protection insurance, formerly known as 'permanent health insurance', is a financial safety net designed to help protect you, your family and your lifestyle in the event that you cannot work and cope financially due to an illness or accidental injury preventing you from working. Most of us need to work to pay the bills.

Tax-free monthly income

Without a regular income you may find it a struggle financially even if you were ill for only a short period, and you could end up using your savings to pay the bills. In the event that you suffered from a serious illness, medical condition or accident, you could even find that you are never able to return to work. Few of us could cope financially if we were off work for more than six to nine months.

Income protection insurance provides a tax-free monthly income for as long as required, up to retirement age, should you be unable to work due to long-term sickness or injury.

By law, your employer must pay most employees statutory sick pay. This will almost certainly be a lot less than your full earnings. Few employers pay for longer periods. If you find yourself in a situation where you are unable to return to work your employer could even stop paying you altogether and terminate your employment. After that, you would probably have to rely on state benefits. Some employers arrange group income protection insurance for their employees which can pay out an income after the statutory sick period.

Before-tax earnings

Income protection insurance aims to put you back to the position you were in before you were unable to work. It does not allow you to make a profit out of your misfortune. So the maximum amount of income you can replace through insurance is broadly the after- tax earnings you have lost, less an adjustment for state benefits you can claim. This is usually translated into a maximum of 50 per cent to 65 per cent of your before-tax earnings.

If you are self-employed then no work is also likely to mean no income. However, depending on what you do you may have income coming in from earlier work even if you are ill for several months.

The self- employed can take out individual policies rather than business ones but you need to ascertain on what basis the insurer will pay out. A typical basis for payment is your pre-tax share of the gross profit after deduction of trading expenses in the 12 months immediately prior to the date of your incapacity. Some policies operate an average over the last three years as they understand that self- employed people often have a fluctuating income.

The cost of your cover will depend on; your gender, occupation, age, state of health, and whether or not you smoke.

Most comprehensive definitions

The 'occupation class' is used by insurers to decide whether a policyholder is able to return to work. If a policy will pay out only if a policyholder is unable to work in 'any occupation', it might not pay benefits for long – or indeed at all. The most comprehensive definitions are 'Own Occupation' or 'Suited Occupation'.

'Own Occupation' means you can make a claim if you are unable to perform

your own job; however being covered under 'Any Occupation' means that you have to be unable to perform any job, with equivalent earnings to the job you were doing before not taken into account.

You can also usually choose for your cover to remain the same (level cover) or increase in line with inflation (inflation-linked cover):

- **Level cover** - with this cover if you made a claim the monthly income is fixed at the start of your plan and would not change in the future. You remember that this means, if inflation eventually starts to rise that the buying power of your monthly income payments may be reduced over time.
- **Inflation-linked cover** - with this cover if you made a claim the monthly income would go up in line with the Retail Prices Index (RPI).

When you take out cover you usually have the choice of:

- **Guaranteed premiums** - the premiums remain the same all the way throughout the term of your plan. If you have chosen inflation-linked cover, your premiums and cover will automatically go up each year in line with RPI.
- **Reviewable premiums** - this means the premiums you pay can increase or decrease in the future. The premiums will not typically increase or decrease for the first five years of your plan but they may do so at any time after that. If your premiums do go up or down they will not change again for the next 12 months.

How long you have to wait after making a claim will depend on the waiting period. The longer the waiting period you choose, the lower the premium for your cover will be, but you'll have to wait longer after you become unable to work before the payments from the policy are paid to you. Premiums must be paid for the entire term of the plan, including the waiting period.

Depending on your circumstances it is possible that the payments from the plan will affect any state benefits due to you. This will depend on your individual situation and what state benefits you are claiming or intending to claim. If you are unsure whether any state benefits you are receiving will be affected you should seek professional financial advice.

Chapter 4
Building Wealth

The first step to building wealth starts with a disciplined decision to pay yourself first, then compounds with a disciplined investment approach.

When you define your investment objectives the priority of where and how to invest should be guided by your specific goals. It should also naturally encourage you to do more as you see it working – encouraging you to further increase, grow and build your wealth. We can help you secure the financial future that you want to achieve and your lifetime goals, enabling you to structure your finances as tax-efficiently as possible.

There are many different ways to grow your wealth, from ensuring you receive the best rates for short-term cash management, to the more complex undertaking of creating an investment portfolio to grow your wealth for the long term.

A properly crafted wealth management strategy allows you to make informed decisions about the investment choices that are right for you by assessing your life priorities, goals and attitude towards risk for return.

Spreading risk in your portfolio

One of the principal tenets of spreading risk in your portfolio is to diversify your investments. Diversification is the process of investing in areas that have little or no relation to each other.

Diversification helps lessen what's known as 'unsystematic risk', such as reductions in the value of certain investment sectors, regions or asset types in general. However, there are some events and risks that diversification cannot help with – these are referred to as 'systemic risks'.

These include interest rates, inflation, wars and recession. This is important to remember when building your portfolio.

The main ways you can diversify your portfolio

Assets

Having a mix of different asset types will spread risk because their movements are either unrelated or inversely related to each other. It's the old adage of not putting all your eggs in one basket.

Probably the best example of this is shares, equities and bonds. Equities are riskier than bonds and can provide growth in your portfolio but traditionally when the value of shares begins to fall bonds begin to rise, and vice versa.

Therefore, if you mix your portfolio between equities and bonds, you're spreading the risk because when one drops the other should rise to cushion your losses. Other asset types such as property and commodities move independently of each other and investment in these areas can spread risk further.

It takes patience and discipline to implement an effective long-term investment strategy. In identifying and evaluating opportunities, we seek to understand how financial markets behave by observing asset valuations, price momentum, investor sentiment and economic climate as indicators of future investment performance.

Sectors

Once you've decided on the assets you want to hold in your portfolio you can diversify further by investing in different sectors, preferably those that aren't related to each other. The investment world changes constantly so when looking at investing in equity markets it is prudent to invest in different sectors.

For example, some sectors may typically be less volatile which may appeal if you are focused on predictability and capital preservation. Meanwhile, other sectors that have more growth prospects and higher volatility may appeal if you have a higher risk tolerance. Many fund managers also focus on sector-specific investments. In some cases fund managers may only focus on investing in one sector, such as the technology sector or the healthcare sector.

Additionally, some fund managers may invest in a range of sectors and companies, but veer away from certain sectors if they don't like the current prospects for that sector. For example, if the healthcare sector takes a downturn this will not necessarily have an impact on the precious metals sector. This helps to make sure your portfolio is protected from falls in certain industries.

Geography

Investing in different regions and countries can reduce the impact of stock market movements. This means you're not just affected by the economic conditions of one country and one government's fiscal policies.

Many markets are not correlated with each other – if the Asian Pacific stock markets perform poorly, it doesn't necessarily mean that the UK's market will be negatively affected. By investing in different regions and areas, you're spreading the risk that comes from the markets.

Developed markets such as the UK and US are not as volatile as some of those in the Far East, Middle East or Africa. Investing abroad can help you diversify, but you need to be comfortable with the levels of risk that come with them.

Company

It's important not to invest in just one company. Spread your investments across a range of different companies.

The same can be said for bonds and property. One of the ways to do this is via a collective investment scheme. This type of scheme invests in a portfolio of different shares, bonds, properties or currencies to spread risk.

Beware of over-diversification

Holding too many assets might be more detrimental to your portfolio than good. If you over-diversify you may be holding back your capacity for growth, as you'll have such small proportions of your money in different investments that you won't see much in the way of positive results.

Pooled Investments

If you require your money to provide the potential for capital growth or income, or a combination of both, and provided you are willing to accept an element of risk, pooled investments could just be the solution you are looking for.

A pooled investment allows you to invest in a large, professionally managed portfolio of assets with many other investors. As a result of this, the risk is reduced due to the wider spread of investments in the portfolio.

Pooled investments are also sometimes called 'collective investments'. The fund manager will choose a broad spread of instruments in which to invest, depending on their investment remit. The main asset classes available to invest in are shares, bonds, gilts, property and other specialist areas such as hedge funds or 'guaranteed funds'.

Most pooled investment funds are actively managed. The fund manager researches the market and buys and sells assets with the aim of providing a good return for investors, in particular because charges need to be deducted. Trackers tend to have lower charges than actively managed funds. This is because a fund manager running an actively managed fund is paid to invest to do better than the index (beat the market) or to generate a steadier return for investors than tracking the index would achieve. However, active management does not guarantee that the fund will outperform the market or a tracker fund.

A pooled investment allows you to invest in a large, professionally managed portfolio of assets

Unit Trusts

Unit trusts are a collective investment that allows you to participate in a wider range of investments than can normally be achieved on your own with smaller sums of money. Pooling your money with others also reduces the risk.

The unit trust fund is divided into units, each of which represents a tiny share of the overall portfolio. Each day the portfolio is valued which determines the value of the units. When the portfolio value rises, the price of the units increases. When the portfolio value goes down, the price of the units falls.

A fund manager or a team of managers, who will make the investment decisions, runs the unit trust. They invest in stock markets all round the world and for the more adventurous investor there are funds investing in individual emerging markets, such as China, or in the so- called BRIC economies (Brazil, Russia, India and China).

Alternatively, some funds invest in metals and natural resources as well as many putting their money into bonds. Some offer a blend of equities, bonds, property and cash, and are known as balanced funds. If you wish to marry your profits with your principles, you can also invest in an ethical fund.

Some funds invest not in shares directly but in a number of other funds. These are known as 'multi-manager funds'. Most fund managers use their own judgement to assemble a portfolio of shares for their funds. These are known as 'actively managed funds'.

However, a sizeable minority of funds simply aim to replicate a particular index, such as the FTSE all-share index. These are known as 'passive funds' or 'trackers'.

Open-ended investment companies

Open-ended investment companies (OEICs) are stock market-quoted collective investment schemes. Like unit trusts and investment trusts, they invest in a variety of assets to generate a return for investors.

An OEIC, pronounced 'oik', is a pooled collective investment vehicle in company form. They may have an umbrella fund structure allowing for many sub-funds with different investment objectives.

This means you can invest for income and growth in the same umbrella fund, moving your money from one sub-fund to another as your investment priorities or circumstances change. OEICs may also offer different share classes for the same fund.

By being 'open ended', OEICs can expand and contract in response to demand, just like unit trusts. The share price of an OEIC is the value of all the underlying investments divided by the number of shares in issue.

As an open-ended fund, the fund gets bigger and more shares are created as more people invest. The fund shrinks and shares are cancelled as people withdraw their money.

You may invest into an OEIC through a Stocks & Shares New Individual Savings Account (NISA). Each time you invest in an OEIC fund, you will be allocated a number of shares.

You can choose either income or accumulation shares, depending on whether you are looking for your investment to grow or to provide you with income, providing they are available for the fund you want to invest in.

Investment Trusts

Investment trusts are based upon fixed amounts of capital divided into shares. This makes them closed ended, unlike the open-ended structure of unit trusts. They can be one of the easiest and most cost-effective ways to invest in the stock market. Once the capital has been divided into shares, you can purchase the shares. When an investment trust sells shares it is not taxed on any capital gains it has made. By contrast, private investors are subject to capital gains tax when they sell shares in their own portfolio.

Another major difference between investment trusts and unit trusts is that investment trusts can borrow money for their investments, known as 'gearing up', whereas unit trusts cannot. Gearing up can work either to the advantage or to disadvantage of investment trusts, depending on whether the stock market is rising or falling.

Investment trusts can also invest in unquoted or unlisted companies which may not be trading on the stock exchange either because they don't wish to or because they don't meet the given criteria. However, this facility combined with the ability to borrow money for investments can make investment trusts more volatile.

The net asset value (NAV) is the total market value of all the trust's investments and assets minus any liabilities. The NAV per share is the net asset value of the trust divided by the number of shares in issue. The share price of an investment trust depends on the supply and demand for its shares in the stock market. This can result in the price being at a 'discount' or a 'premium' to the NAV per share.

A trust's share price is said to be at a discount when the market price of the trust's shares is less than the NAV per share. This means that investors are able to buy shares in the investment trust at less than the underlying stock market value of the trust's assets.

A trust's shares are said to be at a premium when the market price is more than the NAV per share. This means that investors are buying shares in the trust at a higher price than the underlying stock market value of the trust's assets. The movement in discounts and premiums is a useful way to indicate the market's perception of the potential performance of a particular trust or the market where it invests. Discounts and premiums are also one of the key differences between investment trusts and unit trusts or OEICs.

Investment Bonds

An investment bond is a single premium life insurance policy and is a potentially tax-efficient way of holding a range of investment funds in one place. They can be a good way of allowing you to invest in a mixture of investment funds that are managed by professional investment managers.

Each bond is usually designed to provide benefits for different types of investors but a common element is that they aim to produce long-term capital growth and/or generate a long-term return. When you invest in a bond, you will be allocated a certain number of units in the funds of your choice or those set out by the conditions of the bond.

Each fund invests in a range of assets and the price of your units will normally rise and fall in line with the value of these assets. Investment bonds are single premium life insurance policies, meaning that a small element of life insurance is provided. This is paid out after your death.

No capital gains tax is paid on the gains that you make, and you do not pay basic rate income tax on any income.

As a higher-rate taxpayer, you may become liable to income tax at a rate equal to the difference between the basic rate and the higher rates (20%), but not until you cash in your bonds or make partial withdrawals of over 5% per annum of your original investment.

This is because there is a special rule that allows you to make annual withdrawals from your bonds of up to 5% for 20 years without any immediate tax liability. It is possible to carry these 5% allowances forward, so if you make no withdrawals one year, you can withdraw 10% of your investment the next without triggering a tax charge.

Offshore Investments

For the appropriate investor looking to achieve capital security, growth or income, there are a number of advantages to investing offshore, particularly concerning utilising the tax deferral benefits. You can defer paying tax for the lifetime of the investment, so your investment rolls up without tax being deducted, but you still have to pay tax at your highest rate when you cash the investment in. As a result, with careful planning a variety of savers could put offshore investments to good use.

The investment vehicles are situated in financial centres located outside the United Kingdom and can add greater diversification to your existing portfolio. Cash can also be held offshore in deposit accounts, providing you with the choice about when you repatriate your money to the UK, perhaps to add to a retirement fund or to gift to children or grandchildren. Those who work overseas or have moved abroad to enjoy a different lifestyle often want to pay as little tax as is legally possible.

Many offshore funds offer tax deferral. The different types of investment vehicles available offshore include offshore bonds that allow the investor to defer tax within the policy until benefits are taken, rather than be subject to a basic rate tax liability within the underlying funds. This means that if you are a higher rate tax payer in the UK, you could wait until your tax status changes before bringing your funds (and the gains) back into the UK.

The wide choice of different investment types available include offshore redemption policies, personalised policies, offshore unit trusts and OEICs. You may also choose to have access to investments or savings denominated in another currency.

Many banks, insurance companies and asset managers in offshore centres are subsidiaries of major UK, US and European institutions. If you decide to move abroad you may not pay any tax at all when you cash in an offshore investment, although this depends on the rules of your new country.

With regards to savings and taxation, what applies to you in your specific circumstances is generally determined by the UK tax regulations and whatever tax treaties exist between the UK and your host country. The UK has negotiated treaties with most countries so that UK expats in those countries are not taxed twice. If a non-domiciled UK resident is employed by a non-UK resident employer and performs all of their duties outside the UK, the income arising is only subject to UK tax if it is received in or remitted to the UK.

Investor compensation schemes tend not to be as developed as in the UK, so you should always obtain professional advice to ensure that you fully understand each jurisdiction. It is also important to ensure that you are investing in an offshore investment that is appropriate for the level of risk you wish to take.

If you are an expatriate you should find out if you are aware of all the investment opportunities available to you and that you are minimising your tax liability.

Investing money offshore is a very complex area of financial planning and you should always obtain professional advice. Currency movements can also affect the value of an offshore investment.

Chapter 5
Managing Money

Creating a diverse investment portfolio – how to work out your own investment style when things aren't black and white.

'Don't put all your eggs in the same basket' is probably the best-known proverb advising investors about the importance of portfolio diversification to spread and reduce risk.

The major advantage of portfolio diversification is its ability to protect your entire portfolio from volatility associated to various asset classes. In this guide, we look at ways to protect your portfolio by spreading your risk across several different asset classes and some of the many different assets in which you can invest, each with different risk characteristics.

Whilst the risks attributable to assets cannot be avoided, when managed collectively as part of a diversified portfolio, they can be diluted. Individual assets have a bearing on the overall level of risk you are exposed to and the correlation between the assets has an even greater bearing. This guide considers how a well-constructed investment portfolio should be diversified in a variety of ways, including overall investment style, number of individual asset classes, spread of geographical allocation and the approach of the fund manager.

Is it time to review your investment portfolio?

Creating and maintaining the right investment portfolio plays a vital role in securing your financial future. Whether you are looking to invest for income or growth, we can provide the quality advice, comprehensive investment solutions and ongoing service to help you achieve your financial goals. Please contact us to discuss your requirements – we look forward to hearing from you.

Portfolio Diversification - Managing the risks you are exposed to in order to avoid suffering losses to your capital

Whether you're planning to start investing your money, or even if you're already a seasoned investor, it's crucial to make sure you manage the risks you are exposed to in order to avoid suffering losses to your capital. The key is to build a diverse portfolio with a mix of different investments that makes sense for your attitude to risk.

A balanced investment portfolio will contain a mix of equities (shares in companies), government and corporate bonds (loans to governments or companies), property, and cash.

Assets moving independently

Having a mix of different asset types will help you spread risk. It's the old adage of not putting all your eggs in one basket. The theory behind this approach is that the values of different assets can move independently and often for different reasons.

Shares move in line with the fortunes and prospects of companies. By getting the right asset allocation, you could make a healthy return plus you'll also be protecting yourself against the worst downturns in individual markets.

Different investment sectors

Say you held shares in a UK bank in 2006. Your investment may have been very rewarding so you decided to buy more shares in other banks. When the credit crunch hit the following year, sparking the banking crisis, the value of your shares in this sector (financials) would have tumbled.

To avoid this, once you've decided on the assets you want in your portfolio, you can diversify further by investing in different sectors, preferably those that aren't highly correlated to each other.

For example, if the banking sector suffers a downturn, this will not necessarily have an impact on the precious metals sector. This helps to make sure your portfolio is protected from dips in certain industries.

Some investors will populate their portfolios with individual company shares directly, but others will gain access to different sectors through managed funds like unit trusts and OEICs (open-ended investment companies).

Stock market movements

Investing in different regions and countries can reduce the impact of stock market movements. This means you're not just affected by the economic conditions of one country and one government's economic policies.

Different markets are not always highly correlated with each other – if the Japanese stock market performs poorly, it doesn't necessarily mean that the UK's market will be negatively affected.

However, you need to be aware that diversifying in different geographical regions can add extra risk to your investment. Developed markets like the UK and US are not as volatile as those in emerging markets like Brazil, Russia, India and China. Investing abroad can help you diversify, but you need to be comfortable with the levels of risk involved.

Range of different companies

Don't just invest in one company. It might hit bad times or even fail. Spread your investments across a range of different companies. The same can be said for bonds and property. One of the best ways to do this is via a unit trust or OEIC fund. They will invest in a basket of different shares, bonds, properties or currencies to spread risk around. In the case of equities, this might mean 40 to 60 shares in one country, stock market or sector.

With a bond fund you might be invested in 200 different bonds. This will be much more cost effective than recreating it on your own and will help diversify your portfolio.

Capacity for growth

Holding too many assets might be more detrimental to your portfolio than good. If you over diversify you might not end up losing much money, but you may be holding back your capacity for growth, as you'll have such small proportions of your money in different investments to see much in the way of positive results.

It's usually recommended that you hold no more than 30 investments (be it shares or bonds). If you're investing in funds, 15 to 20 should be a maximum.

Finally, for many investors – especially those without the time, confidence or knowledge to make their own investment decisions – seek professional financial advice.

The contents of this book provide information on the matters you may want to consider when reviewing your financial affairs and do not constitute advice. Hartey Wealth Management is authorised and regulated by the Financial Conduct Authority and can provide formal advice if required.

There are references to Tax rates, reliefs and regulations in the book. These were those applicable at the time of publication (December 2015) and are subject to change

Chapter 6
Principles of Diversification

Minimising exposure to volatility and market setbacks

Investing would be easy if markets rose in a straight line. Unfortunately, that is rarely the case. Over the long term assets such as shares and bonds have tended to produce positive returns, but there have been several bumps along the way. In any event, past performance of investments cannot be taken as a guide to their future performance.

There are steps investors can take to minimise their exposure to volatility and market setbacks. One of the most important considerations is to apply the principles of diversification, or spreading your money across a range of assets rather than sticking with one type of investment.

By not putting all your eggs in one basket, you reduce the impact of losses on your overall portfolio. However, investors should bear in mind that a diversified approach would also limit the potential for gains from the rise in a single investment's value.

Returns for investors

Funds make it easy for investors to build a diversified portfolio by reducing the volatility and potential gains and losses associated with individual shares. A typical fund manager investing in UK companies may hold perhaps 30 or 40 different shares in a single fund.

Shares can be volatile and may fall in value. Indeed, during a crisis, all the shares in an index tend to fall together. However, it is less likely that shares in 30 or 40 companies will perform in the same way over time.

Some may perform strongly, while others may not. By holding a number of individual assets, funds tend to smooth out long-term returns for investors.

Single asset class

Investing in different assets, including shares, bonds, property or cash further improves the level of diversification in your overall portfolio. Some funds hold a single asset class, such as shares, while multi-asset funds contain a range of these assets in a single portfolio that is overseen by a fund manager.

Asset classes offer different potential returns based on varying degrees of risk.

For example, shares have historically produced higher returns, but pose a higher risk of capital losses. Bonds generally produce lower returns but with a lower risk of losses.

In addition, assets can react in different ways to the same market forces. Assets that move in opposite directions in response to the same economic changes or market forces are described as having a low or negative correlation.

Offset by gains

When these assets are held together within a diversified portfolio, losses in one part of the portfolio are likely to be offset by gains elsewhere. For example, the prospect of higher inflation is often detrimental to the bond market. The income available from bonds is usually fixed, and is therefore less valuable when inflation is rising.

By contrast, stock markets have tended to cope better with higher inflation, partly because companies can put up prices to combat it, which in turn is reflected in their share prices. Likewise, the value of gold has tended to rise during periods of higher inflation as it is traditionally seen as a hedge against rising prices.

Holding a range of asset classes is also important for income-seeking investors, who try to ensure that their income stream remains relatively steady by drawing it from a variety of sources – coupons from bonds, dividends from companies, rents from commercial property and so on. That way, if one asset class is hit by a change in the economic environment, investors would not expect to see their income stream evaporate.

Types of assets

Diversification doesn't only apply to the types of assets in your portfolio, but also to the regions and sectors within these asset classes. For example, investors could hold shares from different regions of the world, such as the UK and emerging markets, which have tended to produce different returns over time. Emerging markets include Brazil, India and China.

Investors could also look for companies with different market capitalisations, such as large caps and small caps. Broadly speaking, a large-cap company in the UK is considered to be one listed on the FTSE 100 index, which contains the 100 largest companies by market capitalisation. In contrast, small caps in the UK are typically shares listed in the FTSE Small Cap index or on the AIM index of small, fledgling companies.

Shares in fast-growing smaller companies have tended to offer the prospect of stronger returns than larger blue-chip companies, but they are usually much more volatile. As a result, investing in small-cap stocks is riskier than investing in larger companies.

Exchange-traded funds

There are a significant number of funds available that target various asset classes and sectors, from American smaller companies to emerging market bonds. In particular, the growth in low- cost, exchange-traded funds has made it simple and cheap for investors to track a significant range of stock markets and asset classes.

A further way that investors could build a diversified portfolio is to apply different selection criteria when picking assets within any given market. For example, this could mean choosing a mix of defensive and cyclical shares that are more likely to perform differently in response to trends in the wider economy.

Defensive shares, such as utilities or tobacco companies, are those that have a good track record of consistent dividends and stable earnings regardless of the economic climate. As a result, these shares have the potential to perform better than the rest of the market during periods of weaker economic growth.

Strong economic growth

In contrast, the performance of cyclical shares, such as house builder's or luxury retailers, is more closely linked to the economy. These shares have the potential to perform strongly during times of strong economic growth, but often fall in value when the economy is performing less well.

The balance of assets in your overall portfolio should reflect your appetite for risk and reward. Generally speaking, the larger the proportion of equities held in a portfolio, the riskier it is considered to be.

For example, a higher-risk portfolio may hold 50% developed market equities from the UK, US or Europe; 20% emerging market equities; 10% bonds; and the remainder commodities, property and cash.

Lower-risk portfolio

By contrast, a lower-risk portfolio may only contain 15% developed market equities, 5% emerging market equities, 20% bonds, 40% cash and the remainder in property and commodities. A balanced portfolio would be somewhere between these extremes.

Multi-asset funds can offer a one-stop shop for investors looking to build a diversified portfolio from scratch, combining a range of assets from different regions and sectors to reduce volatility and the risk of potential losses.

Investors should choose a multi-asset fund to match their risk appetite based on the proportion of shares in its portfolio. Multi-asset funds commonly feature labels such as adventurous, balanced, cautious or absolute return, representing different levels of risk, while others feature a numerical risk rating.

Multi-asset funds

The Investment Association, an industry trade body, groups multi-asset funds into four categories, from 'Mixed Investment 0-35% Shares', which are lower risk, to 'Flexible Investment', the riskiest category of multi-asset funds which can hold up to 100% in shares.

Some draw upon several managers as well as asset classes. These multi- manager funds can benefit from the investment styles of a wider range of experts, and they can also give you access to managers who may not normally be marketed to private investors.

Maintaining a diversified portfolio should help smooth out returns for investors. It can protect you from some of the worst market declines but still allow you to benefit from potential upswings in performance. Diversification, in short, should make investing a less nail-biting experience.

Please remember that regardless of whether you diversify, the values of all investments can fall as well as rise, and you may get back less than you invested. Past performance is not a reliable guide to future performance.

Chapter 7
Investment Portfolio

Every investor is unique, but everyone faces the same trade-off between risk and reward.

The best place to start when you are looking to build a diverse investment portfolio is to ask yourself why you're building a portfolio. For most of us, the central task is to build a pot of money that involves you, the investor, taking some risk over the long term, at the end of which you will have ideally built up a sizeable portfolio of diversified assets that will last you through to your retirement years.

Some investors don't have such a long-term objective and are thus less willing to take on risks. They might for instance, only be saving for ten years to cover school fees. Alternatively, they may already be in retirement and need to generate an income while preserving their money against inflation, even at the cost of future opportunity. For both of these latter groups a sensible investment strategy is likely to involve a relatively low level of 'risky' assets such as equities.

Above-average returns

Therefore, every investor is unique but everyone faces the same trade-off between risk and reward. In simple terms, you can't hope for long-term, above-average returns unless you are willing to take on more risk. This might sound like a simple idea, but an astonishingly large number of investors persist in the myth that double-digit year-on-year growth is possible without risking the loss of a substantial chunk of their assets.

Investing in equities is only a viable option for the long term (at least five years, if not ten), and if capital preservation is your primary objective, you should probably steer clear of stocks and shares and stick to less risky, less exciting assets such as bonds and cash.

Perceptions of risk

As you grow older and your requirements change (as well as your perceptions of risk), your portfolio of assets must also adapt. To give you an idea of how your portfolio might change, lifecycle or lifestyle funds have been developed. These funds mix equities, bonds and property assets in different proportions according to how close the holders are to retirement (or how far beyond it).

Simply put, they start with 100% of assets in risky equities for a worker in his or her thirties, and then end with a portfolio where 75% is allocated to low-risk bonds for an investor into his or her retirement.

Old rule of thumb

This is known in the investment industry as 'life styling'. It's a term for a very old rule of thumb: subtract your age from 100, and that's how much you should hold in equities if appropriate to your particular situation. So if you're 30, have 70% of your investment portfolio in equities. If you're 60, have 40% in stocks and shares.

It is vitally important that any rearrangement of your portfolio is controlled and measured. Never forget that every time you buy and sell assets, some of your money is lost in fees. Virtually every analysis of historical returns suggests that investors shouldn't over-trade, shouldn't try to time the markets and absolutely should avoid turning into speculators.

Long-term strategy

Instead, the consensus is that private investors should work out a long-term strategy, build a diversified, robust portfolio, and then sit tight as a buy-and- hold investor.

The basics of building an investment portfolio are surprisingly simple. Work out your own investing style, and then make sure that your diversified mixture of asset classes mirrors your own risk-reward trade off.

Higher risk levels

If you're willing to embrace higher-risk levels and won't need the money for a while, think about tilting your portfolio towards shares. If you only have a narrow time horizon for what you want to achieve from your investment, give more weight to bonds and cash.

And don't get too carried away: keep the underlying funds within your portfolio simple and cheap, and don't over-trade.

Reducing Investment Risk - Choosing a broad spread of instruments in which to invest

If you require your money to provide the potential for capital growth or income, or a combination of both, and provided you are willing to accept an element of risk, pooled investments allow you to invest in a large, professionally managed portfolio of assets with many other investors. As a result of this, the risk is reduced due to the wider spread of investments in the portfolio.

Collective investments

Pooled investments are also sometimes called 'collective investments'. The fund manager will choose a broad spread of instruments in which to invest, depending on their investment remit.

The main asset classes available to invest in are shares, bonds, gilts, property and other specialist areas such as hedge funds or 'guaranteed funds'.

Passively managed

Trackers on the other hand, are passively managed, aiming to track the market in which they are invested. For example, a FTSE 100 tracker would aim to replicate the movement of the FTSE 100 (the index of the largest 100 UK companies). They might do this by buying the equivalent proportion of all the shares in the index. For technical reasons, the return is rarely identical to the index, in particular because charges need to be deducted.

A higher return on your Investment

Invest as much of your annual ISA allowance as you like in either a Stocks & Shares ISA or a Cash ISA, or any mixture of the two. Some people never look beyond Cash Individual Savings Accounts (ISAs), but by using Stocks & Shares ISAs too, you could get a higher return on your investment. Stocks & Shares ISAs can contain shares, bonds and investment funds. There are no restrictions about where in the world you can invest: it does not have to be all in the UK.

ISA Allowance

Following 1 July 2014, you can now invest as much of your annual ISA allowance as you like in either a Stocks & Shares ISA or a Cash ISA, or any mixture of the two, as long as you don't exceed the annual limit. The annual limit is currently £15,240 for the 2015/16 tax year.

Building up a reserve of ready money before heading into riskier assets like shares is good practice, and it has been recommended that people try and maintain three to six months' worth of income saved as cash, which can be used for emergencies.

Financial plan

At this point having created a buffer, the next step is to decide on a financial plan, determining what your investment objectives are, your financial capability and, most importantly, how much risk you are willing to take.

Whatever your age, risk profile and wider portfolio, it is inadvisable to put all of your money in the same asset class.

So don't invest everything in the UK stock market or US government bonds. Diversification is one of the first principles of investing.

Lower-risk options

For those who prefer a lower-risk option, you can take various options besides simply leaving all your money in cash.

You could find a fund that invests in fixed-interest securities, known as 'bonds'. These are less risky than shares but may perform better than cash, especially with today's current low interest rates.

If you want to take as much risk off the table as possible while still using your entire ISA allowance, it may make sense to leave the maximum amount in cash and invest the other funds in government or corporate bonds.

Although bond funds are low risk, it is still worth noting that the value of your investment may go down as well as up, and you may get back less than you put in. That said, the best bond funds have an excellent record at preserving investors' capital and have grown it significantly too.

Remain defensively positioned

If you are seeking a higher return on your investment but still want to remain defensively positioned, you could start looking at the stock market.

Accessing stocks and shares (or 'equities') through funds enables you to invest mainly in larger companies in developed markets, such as the UK, US and Western Europe, or a defensive global fund. 'Income' funds that invest in companies that pay dividends can be a good choice, because strong companies can maintain dividends even in bad times when their profits and share prices are falling.

Your main choice will be between actively managed and passively managed funds. A fund manager who tries to beat the market by making better investing decisions than everyone else runs active funds. Passive funds, which have lower fees and charges, try to match the performance of a well-established index, such as the FTSE 100.

If you go with an active fund, be sure to check the fund's reputation and performance, but bear in mind this is not necessarily a guide to the future.

With a passive fund, the important things are that it tracks its index accurately and has low fees.

Pound cost averaging

We've all heard that stock markets can be volatile and that the value of investments can go down, but there can be a positive side to these market conditions by regularly saving into funds through a Stocks & Shares ISA, a benefiting from a concept known as 'pound cost averaging'.

Pound cost averaging is about regular saving. When investing, it's always best to buy at the cheapest point – when prices hit the bottom. Yet predicting that point is extremely difficult. As a result, many investors miss it and act when the market starts rising.

However, you can even out the ups and downs when you make regular payments into a Stocks & Shares ISA investment, instead of paying in a one-off sum. By investing regularly – throughout the year, let's say monthly – you spread the risk.

The money in your fund is used to buy units. If the unit price at that point is lower than the average price over a period of time, this can result in greater potential value. Remember though that, as with all forms of investing nothing is guaranteed. You could gain less or lose more than if you had invested in one lump sum.

Potentially higher return

For those who are prepared to take more risk in order to get a potentially higher return, a move away from income- producing assets (such as bonds or the shares of big companies) towards capital growth may be worth considering. If you are willing to take an aggressive approach, it may be worth looking at small- to mid-cap companies and emerging market funds.

Bear in mind though that you may need to change your asset allocation over time. As retirement approaches for instance, you might want to use your ISA as a source of additional income (remember, you do not have to pay tax on any income you take out of your ISA, but income from a pension is liable for tax). In your fifties and sixties, you may want to switch some of your investments from stocks and shares to bonds, for example.

Ultimately, while ISAs offer welcome tax-efficient incentives to savers, the rules of the market still apply. All the tax exemptions under the sun won't return your cash if you make some awful investment decisions. After all, it's just a wrapper – it's what you put in it that counts.

Open-Ended Funds – Professionally managed collective investment funds

Unit trusts and open-ended investment companies (OEICs) are professionally managed collective investment funds. Managers pool money from many investors and buy shares, bonds, property or cash assets and other investments. An open-ended fund could be visualised as a big pool of money – the money belongs to thousands of small investors.

The fund, or pool, is divided into units. Investors can buy or sell units at any time. As people buy units the pool gets bigger, as they sell them it gets smaller (this is what is meant by the term 'open-ended').

The unit price is calculated daily by working out the value of all holdings in the fund – cash, shares, bonds or whatever – and dividing it by the number of units.

A fund manager makes decisions about what to invest the money in within the scope of the agreed investment mandate. The objective is to provide returns to the fund's investors, either in the form of capital growth (an increase in the price per unit) or income (dividends paid to the unit holders in proportion to the number of units they hold).

The point of investing in an open-ended fund is that you believe a fund manager can make better investment decisions than you can on your own.

There are two main kinds of open-ended funds available to investors in the UK:
- Unit trusts – their units are dual-priced, there is a (higher) buy price and a (lower) sell price. If you invest in these it is important to realise that you are in effect being charged an additional fee by the fund manager: the difference between the buy price and the sell price (sometimes called the bid and offer price)
- Open-ended investment companies (OEICs) – these have a single unit price. Most unit trusts have now been converted to OEICs

In all other important respects unit trusts and OEICs work in exactly the same way. In fact, the term 'unit trusts' is sometimes used loosely to refer to both unit trusts and OEIC.

Forward pricing

Another important feature of open-ended funds is forward pricing. This mechanism means that when you place an order to buy or sell units in a fund you will not be sure exactly what the unit price is until the deal is done.

Say the fund is priced daily at 12 noon. If you place an order at 10am on Wednesday to buy or sell units, that order will be carried out after the fund is priced at noon on Wednesday, at the new price.

If you place an order on Wednesday at 4pm, you would have to wait until Thursday at 12 noon for that order to be executed at Thursday's price.

The main purpose of forward pricing is to discourage short-term trading in open-ended funds, which could make life difficult for fund managers.

Investment return

Open-ended funds usually invest in shares (equities) or bonds. They may also invest in derivatives or keep money in cash, but this is mainly to help them manage their portfolios and is not usually expected to produce an investment return.

It is less common for open-ended funds to invest in physical property. This is because units can be bought or redeemed at any time. If a lot of people suddenly wanted to sell their units it would be hard for the fund to sell properties quickly enough to pay them back.

The value of your investments can go down as well as up, and you may get back less than you invested.

Some assets are riskier than others are, but higher risk also gives you the potential to earn higher returns. Before investing make sure you understand what kind of assets the fund invests in and whether that's a good fit for your investment goals, financial situation and attitude to risk.

Building block of many Investor Portfolios

Investing in bonds, pooling your money with thousands of other small investors.

Bonds are debt issued by either a government or a company and are an essential building block of many investors' portfolios. When you buy a bond you are effectively extending a loan to the issuer of the bond.

The issuer agrees to pay you a set interest rate (the 'coupon') at a set number of times per year before returning your initial 'loan' in its entirety at the date set out at the issuance of the bond (the 'maturity date').

If the company (or country) defaults, you're not going to get that loan back.

Following the introduction of the Order Book for Retail Bonds (ORB) by the London Stock Exchange it's also worth noting that both individual bonds and bond funds can be included in a Stocks & Shares ISA.

Real value of money

People invest in bonds for a steady income and do not usually expect growth on their investment. Their capital tends to be fairly safe, although some bonds are safer than others. The less safe a bond is perceived to be, the higher the coupon: it has to compensate investors for the risk they are taking.

Sterling is currency risk. If you buy a Japanese bond and the value of the yen falls against the pound, you'll be sitting on a loss in sterling terms.

Bonds fall into two main types: government bonds and corporate bonds. Government bonds have colourful names depending on which government issued them. UK government bonds are gilts, US government bonds are treasuries and German bonds are bunds.

Ratings agencies rate both government and corporate bonds for the benefit of investors; however, they can be wrong, as witnessed during the financial crisis of 2008.

Equities – a relative safe haven against global economic problems. Of course, this depends on which equities and which bonds; a high-yield bond may be riskier than a defensive blue-chip equity.

Chapter 8
Asset Allocation

Deciding how to weight your portfolio

Asset allocation is the bedrock of successful investing. The challenge for investors lies in deciding exactly how much to allocate to each asset class.

Assets classes

Once you understand your investment goals and risk tolerance, the challenge lies in deciding how to weight your portfolio. It should have exposure to the main assets classes: cash, bonds, equities (shares in companies) and property.

The idea is that those with a lower risk tolerance will overweigh in assets offering more certain returns, like cash and bonds. And those less averse to risk and with longer investment time horizons might invest in more volatile assets, like shares, that have a higher potential return.

However, the principles of diversification mean that this minimalist approach is risky. For example, within the shares asset class you will want exposure to investments that focus on growth as well as dividends. And it is difficult to achieve this through just one fund. On the other hand, the ease with which we can buy funds now means that investors must be careful – avoid buying too many when structuring your portfolio, as they may overlap with each other.

Potential returns

The potential returns available from different kinds of investment and the risks involved can also change over time as a result of economic, political and regulatory developments, as well as a host of other factors.

Society savings accounts and money market funds are investment vehicles that invest in securities such as short-term bonds to enable institutions and larger personal investors to invest cash for the short term.

Money held in the bank is arguably more secure than any of the other asset classes, but it is also likely to provide the poorest return over the long term. Indeed, with inflation currently above the level of interest provided by many accounts, the real value of cash held on deposit is falling.

The effects of inflation and tax could erode your money. If your savings are taxed that return will be reduced even further.

Bonds

Bonds are effectively IOUs issued by governments or companies. In return for your initial investment, the issuer pays a pre-agreed regular return (the 'coupon') for a fixed term at the end of which it agrees to return your initial investment.

Depending on the financial strength of the issuer bonds can be very low or relatively high risk, and the level of interest paid varies accordingly with higher-risk issuers needing to offer more

Equities

- Economic background – companies perform best in an environment of healthy economic growth, modest inflation and low interest rates.
  - o A poor outlook for growth could suggest waning demand for the company's products or services.
  - o High inflation could affect companies in the form of increased input prices, although in some cases companies may be able to pass this on to consumers.

o Rising interest rates could put strain on companies that have borrowed heavily to grow the business

• Investor sentiment – as higher risk assets, equities are susceptible to changes in investor sentiment. Deterioration in risk appetite normally sees share prices fall, while a turn to positive sentiment can see equity markets rise sharply

Property

In investment terms, property normally means commercial real estate – offices, warehouses, retail units and the like. Unlike the assets we have mentioned so far, properties are unique – only one fund can own a particular office building or shop.

The performance of these assets can sometimes be dominated by changes.

Economic background – companies perform best in an environment of healthy economic growth, modest inflation and low interest rates. A poor outlook for growth could suggest waning demand for the company's products or services. High inflation could affect companies in the form of increased input prices, although in some cases, companies may be able to pass this on to consumers. Rising interest rates could put strain on companies that have borrowed heavily to grow the business.

The more normal state of affairs is for rental income to be the main driver of commercial property returns. Owners of property can enhance the income potential and capital value of their assets by undertaking refurbishment work or other improvements. Indeed, without such work property can quickly become uncompetitive and run down.

When managed properly the relatively stable nature of property's income return is key to its appeal for investors.

Mix of assets

In order to maximise the performance potential of a diversified portfolio, managers actively change the mix of assets they hold to reflect the prevailing market conditions. These changes can be made at a number of levels including the overall asset mix, the target markets within each asset class and the risk profile of underlying funds within markets.

As a rule, an environment of positive or recovering economic growth and healthy risk appetite would be likely to prompt an increased weighting in equities and a lower exposure to bonds. Within these baskets of assets, the manager might also move into more aggressive portfolios when markets are doing well, and ones that are more cautious when conditions are more difficult. Geographical factors such as local economic growth, interest rates and the political background will also affect the weighting between markets within equities and bonds.

Underlying portfolios

In the underlying portfolios managers will normally adopt a more defensive positioning when risk appetite is low.

For example, in equities, they might have higher weightings in large companies operating in parts of the market that are less reliant on robust economic growth.

Conversely, when risk appetite is abundant, underlying portfolios will tend to raise their exposure to more economically sensitive parts of the market and to smaller companies.

Some investors choose to build their own portfolios, either by buying shares, bonds and other assets directly or by combining funds investing in each area. However, this is a very time-consuming approach, and it can be difficult to keep abreast of developments in the markets, whilst also researching all the funds on offer.

For this reason, most investors prefer to place their portfolio into the hands of professional managers and to entrust the selection of those managers to a professional financial adviser.

Investing for Income - Alternatives for income-seekers during a period of low interest rates

One of the tools available to the Bank of England to stimulate the economy is interest rates.

Lower interest rates mean that it is cheaper to borrow money and people have more to spend, hopefully stimulating the economy and reducing the risk of deflation.

This is why the Bank of England has aggressively cut them. With interest rates at their lowest levels in history, those relying on the interest from bank or building society accounts to supplement their income potentially face a problem. Indeed, once tax and inflation are taken into account, for many their capital on deposit is at risk of losing money in real terms.

If you are an income seeker much will come down to your attitude to risk. If you want no or very low risk, you may wish to consider a traditional cash bank account and accept that income levels are likely to remain low for the foreseeable future. However, if you're further up the risk scale you may wish to consider some of these alternatives.

Gilts

If you're willing to take on a slightly higher degree of risk and you need the extra income, you may wish to consider gilts (or gilt-edged stocks), which are bonds issued by the Government and pay a fixed rate of interest twice a year.

Gilts involve more risk than cash because there's a chance the Government won't be able to pay you back. It's highly unusual for a government to default on a debt or on the interest payments, so they have been considered safe. However, in this current economic climate this risk increases.

You are not guaranteed to get all your capital back under all circumstances. Not all gilts are bought from the Government and held to maturity: some are bought and sold along the way so there's a chance for their value, and the value of gilt funds to rise and fall.

There are other types such as index-linked gilts, which form the largest part of the gilt portfolio after conventional gilts. Here, the coupon is related to movements in the Retail Prices Index (RPI) and is linked to inflation.

Corporate bonds

Next along the risk scale if you are looking for a higher yield are corporate bonds. These are issued by companies and have features that are exactly the same as gilts except that instead of lending money to the Government you're lending to a company. The risk lies in the fact that companies may go bust and the debt may not be repaid.

They have a nominal value (usually £100), which is the amount that will be returned to the investor on a stated future date (the 'redemption date').

They also pay a stated interest rate each year, usually fixed. The value of the bonds themselves can rise and fall; however, the fact that bonds are riskier at the moment means companies are paying more in order to induce people to buy their debt.

There are an increasing number of global bond funds entering the market that may enable you to get value from a number of different markets.

Equity income

If your primary objective is the preservation of income, you may not consider the stock market as the obvious place for your money.

However, for investors who are prepared to see their investments fluctuate in value while hopefully providing a stable income that grows over time, you may wish to consider equity income funds. These invest in shares, focusing on the big blue-chip firms that have a track record.

Regular Portfolio Reviews

Considering the suitability of your investments

It is important to carry out regular portfolio reviews to consider the suitability of your investments and to make sure that any changes in your attitude to risk are accurately reflected. Over time, your attitude to risk is likely to change. If you are approaching retirement, for example, you may want to preserve capital or generate an income, while if you are investing for growth, you may need to take on more risk to potentially boost returns.

You should ask two key questions yourself: firstly, 'How much capital can you afford to lose?', and then, 'How long is your investment horizon?' The general rule is that the more risk you are prepared to take, the greater your potential returns could be. At the same time, however, it is important to realise that there is a greater potential for loss.

Reviewing the amount of risk

As these two factors can change over time, it is crucial that you are able to adjust your portfolio to reflect them. Please remember that the value of your investments and the income received from them may go down as well as up, and you may not get back the full amount invested.

As well as regularly reviewing the amount of risk taken in your portfolio, it is also important to make sure your portfolio remains as diversified as it can be and that it reflects any changes in your investment objectives. The key to building a diversified portfolio is to take a balanced approach. This means combining a range of investments that can help you meet your investment goals within an appropriate level of risk.

Exposure to different markets

Income-seeking stock market investors may want to diversify away from their home UK market to take advantage of dividend opportunities globally.

Meanwhile, in fixed income, the current low yield environment means that investors may need to look across a wider range of global bond sectors and markets to maintain attractive future returns. Either way, you need to make sure you have the right levels of exposure to different markets for the outcomes you're looking for. However, please note that diversification does not guarantee investment returns and does not eliminate the risk of loss.

Investing outside of the UK can involve a higher degree of risk and also involves a degree of exchange rate risk. If you are in any doubt about the suitability of an investment or understanding your risk appetite, please seek professional financial advice.

Chapter 9
Pension Freedom – The most radical reforms of this century

In Budget 2014, Chancellor George Osborne promised greater pension freedom from 6 April 2015. People will be able to access as much or as little of their defined contribution pension as they want and pass on their hard-earned pensions to their families tax-free.

For some people, an annuity may still be the right option, whereas others might want to take their whole tax-free lump sum and convert the rest to drawdown.

Extended choices

'We've extended the choices even further by offering people the option of taking a number of smaller lump sums, instead of one single big lump sum,' Mr Osborne said.

From 6 April 2015, people will be allowed full freedom to access their pension savings at retirement. Pension Freedom Day, as it has been named, is the day that savers can access their pension savings when they want. Each time they do, 25% of what they take out will be tax-free. Under current rules, a 25% withdrawal must be taken as a single lump sum on retirement to be free of tax.

Free to choose

Mr Osborne said, 'People who have worked hard and saved all their lives should be free to choose what they do with their money, and that freedom is central to our long-term economic plan.'

From 6 April 2015, people aged 55 and over can access all or some of their pension without any of the tax restrictions that currently apply. The pension company can choose to offer this freedom to access money, but it does not have to do so.

Accessing money

It will be important to obtain professional financial advice to ensure that you access your money safely, without unnecessary costs and a potential tax bill.

Generally, most companies will allow you to take the full amount out in one go. You can access the first 25% of your pension fund tax-free. The remainder is added to your income for the year, to be taxed at your marginal income tax rate.

This means a non–tax payer could pay 20% or even 40% tax on some of their withdrawal, and basic rate taxpayers might easily slip into a higher rate tax band. For those earning closer to £100,000, they could lose their personal allowance and be subject to a 60% marginal tax charge.

Potential tax bill

If appropriate, it may be more tax- efficient to withdraw the money over a number of years to minimise a potential tax bill. If your pension provider is uncooperative because the contract does not permit this facility, you may want to consider moving pension providers.

You need to prepare and start early to assess your own financial situation. Some providers may take months to process pension transfers, so you'll need time to do your research.

Questions to ask

You will need to ask yourself some important questions. Are there any penalties for taking the money early? Are these worth paying for or can they be avoided by waiting? Are there any special benefits such as, a higher tax-free cash entitlement or guaranteed annuity rates, that would be worth keeping?

If you decide after receiving professional financial advice, that moving providers is the right thing to do, then we can help you search the market for a provider who will allow flexible access.

Importantly, it's not all about the process. You also need to think about the end results.

Withdrawing money

What do you want to do with the money once you've withdrawn it? You may have earmarked some to spend on a treat, but most people want to keep the money saved for their retirement. Paying off debt is usually a good idea.

If you plan just to put the money in the bank, you must remember you maybe be taxed on the interest. With returns on cash at paltry levels, you might be better keeping it in a pension until you need to spend it. Furthermore, this may also save on inheritance tax.

Expect queues as we approach April 2015, as there's likely to be a backlog of people who've put off doing anything with their pension monies.

Those who get through the process quickly and efficiently will be the ones who've done the groundwork.

CLEVER RETIREMENT STRATEGIES

On 10 July 2014, the Office for Budget Responsibility warned that many of us might not be eligible for a State Pension until we reach the age of 70. That's the minimum age the Government will be able to afford to pay our pensions by 2063 if it is also to stop the national debt spiralling out of control.

This milestone could be reached as soon as 2037 – meaning that some people in their late 40s today may have to work to age 70. And if the population ages more quickly than currently forecast, the State Pension age could increase to age 75 in 2064. By then, the UK's official budget watchdog says there could be more than one million people aged over 100 in the UK.

Life expectancy increasing

With life expectancy increasing at a rapid rate, you will probably live for longer than you think and, as such, your pension income will need to last longer. Therefore, it is essential to eke out as much income as possible from your retirement savings and, with interest rates at historical lows, this is no easy task.

It is important to remember that your pension income will not just be a function of the pension vehicle you choose – whether this is an annuity, income drawdown or another arrangement. You can also influence the income you receive in retirement by making clever use of different retirement strategies.

Three retirement strategies to consider

1. Defer your State Pension

Retirement should be a gradual phasing in of income to free up spare time – it does not necessarily have to mean that you stop working or earning. There is no reason why you have to stop working or claim your State Pension when you reach State Pension age – currently 65 for men and 62 for women.

If you put off claiming your State Pension, you can either earn extra State Pension or benefit from a one-off lump sum payment. If you have not yet claimed your State Pension and you want to put off taking it up, you do not need to do anything. Those already drawing their State Pension, but wanting to stop claiming it to earn more income, will have to contact their pension centre.

It is, however, worth noting that the terms for deferring your State Pension are very different for those who reach State Pension age before 6 April 2016 compared to those who reach it afterwards.

For those who reach State Pension age before 6 April 2016 (men aged 64 or more at April 2015 or women aged 62 or more at April 2015), the rate of deferral is very generous – 10.4% per annum plus the inflationary increases. In comparison, the lump sum alternative may be poor value for money.

For people reaching State Pension age after 6 April 2016, the rate of deferral at the time of writing this article had not been set but is expected to be 5% per annum plus inflation, and there will be no lump sum alternative.

2. Use employment to top up your pension

If you are employed, there are a number ways in which you can top up your pension.

Salary sacrifice

Salary sacrifice involves giving up some of your salary in exchange for payments into your pension. This will not only increase your pension contributions and overall pension fund but can also mean savings on income tax and National Insurance. You will receive tax relief, depending on the tax band you fall.

If you are still saving for retirement, it is important that you keep increasing the amount you pay into your pension each year

It is, however, worth remembering that a reduction in your salary could impact your ability to secure a mortgage, as banks and building societies use income to decide on loan eligibility.

Bonus sacrifice

In a similar way to salary sacrifice, you can make potential tax savings by using bonus sacrifice to pay into your pension plan. If you are a high earner, chances are that you receive a basic salary as well as bonus payments.

Typically, you will be offered the chance to sacrifice some of this bonus and instead have that money paid into your pension scheme.

This is arguably one of the most tax- efficient ways of getting extra money into your pension plan, since you are not taxed on the amount of bonus that you give up. Your total income is reduced and therefore you are only taxed on the income you actually receive. The part that goes into your pension is not taxed, as it is instead an employer contribution. This means you save on income tax and National Insurance.

Furthermore, your employer will not pay National Insurance on the amount of bonus given up – usually at 13.8% – and if they wish, they can pass some or all of this saving back to you.

Company share pensions

Those who hold shares in employer share schemes can place these within a Self- Invested Personal Pension (SIPP) and benefit from the tax relief. You can either sell the shares and invest proceeds into your SIPP or move the shares into the SIPP. Once the shares are transferred into a SIPP, any future growth and dividend payments will be tax-efficient.

3. Build in inflation protection

If you are still saving for retirement, it is important that you keep increasing the amount you pay into your pension each year. If you don't, inflation means that your monthly contributions will be worth less every year.

If you expect inflation to rise, then consider investing your pension fund in higher-risk assets such as equities, as rising inflation will eat away at the more cautious investments such as cash, fixed interest and low-risk funds. You will have to take into consideration how many years it will be before you retire and whether you can afford to take the risk of investing in these assets.

Once you reach the point of retirement, you can inflation-proof your income by opting for an inflation-linked annuity, although these usually have a low starting level of income.

Alternatively, you can look at using a drawdown arrangement, usually making use of a multi-asset approach to investment that aims to allow income to be withdrawn while maintaining the real value of your investments.

Under this approach, you won't have a guaranteed income, but you retain ownership and control of your assets while staying abreast of inflation if the investments perform well. However, it is sensible to make sure your essential expenses are covered with a source of secure income where possible.

Closer to retirement

Retirement may be a long way off for you at the moment, but that doesn't mean you should forget about it, and as you get closer it makes sense to have a clearer idea of what you'll need to live on in the future and what your income might be.

Chapter 10
State Pension Changes

Over half of the UK population is unaware of reforms to the State Pension and the impact that could have on them, according to recent research [1]. Among the 55 to 64-year-old age group, 32% are unaware of the changes.

A new single-tier, flat rate State Pension is being introduced which will affect people reaching State Pension age from 6 April 2016 onwards. In May 2014, Parliament agreed the Pensions Act 2014.

State Pension reforms:

* Introduction of a single-tier, flat-rate State Pension, which will replace the basic and additional pensions for people reaching State Pension age from 6 April 2016 onwards.
* Increases in the State Pension age from 66 to 67 between April 2026 and April 2028.
* Making provision for 5-yearly reviews of the State Pension age.

The study found 57% thought the new flat rate State Pension would be worth less than £150 per week – the weekly amount recently set by the government and due to come into effect in April 2016.

The new single-tier pension will only affect people reaching State Pension age from 6 April 2016 onwards.

That is:

* Women born on or after 6 April 1953
* Men born on or after 6 April 1951

Current State Pension will continue

The current State Pension and benefit systems will continue for those who are already pensioners or who reach State Pension age before 6 April 2016. It's the date that you reach State Pension age that's important - not when you start to claim your pension. However, you may be able to make top-ups.

For people who are already receiving their pension or who will reach State Pension age before 6 April 2016, a new scheme starting in October 2015 will allow people to pay a new class of voluntary National Insurance (NI) contributions (called Class 3A).

Additional State Pension boost

This is intended to help people boost their additional State Pension by a maximum of £25 per week. The scheme will be open for a period of 18 months from October 2015. Anyone considering this will need to weigh up the costs of contributions with the likely increase to their pension income.

Pension Credit guarantee will continue to be available under the new system, but those who reach State Pension age on or after 6 April 2016 will not be able to claim savings credit. Housing Benefit will continue (but will be incorporated into Pension Credit in the future) and the system of Council Tax support will also remain.

'Married woman's contributions'

The State Pension is based on your own contributions and in general you will not be able to claim on your spouse or registered civil partner's contributions at retirement or if you are widowed or divorced. However, if you're widowed you may be able to inherit part of your partner's additional State Pension already built up.

There is also provision under the new system for women who paid the reduced rate 'married woman's contributions' to use these contributions towards the new State Pension.

The flat rate State Pension is a key part of government reforms to the UK's retirement planning and will benefit savers by demonstrating the value of pension saving.

If you are not on course to receive a full State Pension on your own contributions you may be able to increase your entitlement – for example by paying voluntary NI contributions or if you are eligible for credits.

Underestimating State Pension values

Although most of the respondents underestimated the value of their State Pension and admitted to not knowing the details of the reforms, two thirds of men and women regard it as important to their retirement income planning.

Of those surveyed, just under half of 55 to 64-year-olds were unsure as to whether or not they would be better off under the new State Pension system compared to the current one.

Key part of government reforms

The flat rate State Pension is a key part of government reforms to the UK's retirement planning and will benefit savers by demonstrating the value of pension saving. However, just under half of those aged between 55 and 64 who are about to retire have no understanding of whether or not they will be better off.

Source data: [1] Research for MetLife conducted online between 21–22 May 2014 among a nationally representative sample of 2,038 adults by independent market research firm

8 Steps to a Brighter Retirement

1. From 6 April 2015, you can use your pension savings in any way you like. The first 25% can be taken as tax-free cash and the remainder used as you wish (all income or capital withdrawals subject to your marginal rate of tax at the time).
2. Consider when you want or need to take your benefits – from both state and any private pensions. You don't have to use them at 'traditional' retirement ages or when you stop working.
3. If you have a small pension pot (individually below £10,000 or up to three valued at less than £30,000), you may be able to take the whole pot as a lump sum under the current 'triviality' rules (from 6 April 2015, you will be able to take the whole pension as cash, subject to marginal tax rates at the time).
4. If an income is important to you, consider all the different options available to you, such as an annuity, an investment-linked annuity and income drawdown. Each of these comes with different risks – income from drawdown or an investment-linked annuity could fall in future.
5. Consider the 'cost of delay' – if you are looking for a guaranteed lifetime income, then an annuity could be your safest option. By delaying any decision until next year, you are missing out on income this year, which could take many years to make up.
6. Think about how much flexibility you need over your income, bearing in mind you may be in retirement for 20 plus years, and if you want to protect your spouse or partner when you die.
7. With annuities, the income is guaranteed but may come with the risk of inflation, which means the income you receive may not buy as much in the future. You can protect your income from inflation but this comes at a cost.
8. If you buy an annuity, don't automatically purchase it from the company you saved with.

Make sure you shop around other providers, giving full information about your health and lifestyle – this can help you get a substantially bigger income.

Pensions for the self-employed
Building funds for your retirement

If you're self-employed, saving into a pension can be a more difficult habit to develop than it is for people in employment. There are no employer contributions, and irregular income patterns can make regular saving difficult. Nevertheless, preparing for retirement is crucial for you too.

Don't rely on the State Pension

If you're self-employed, you're entitled to the basic State Pension in the same way as anyone else. The full basic State Pension is currently set at £115.95 a week. The amount of State Pension you receive depends on your National Insurance contributions, and sometimes those of your current or former spouse or registered civil partner. To get the full amount, you need 30 qualifying years of National Insurance contributions or credits (more if you reached State Pension age before 6th April 2010).

However, that's the extent of your entitlement to the State Pension – you can only claim the additional State Pension if you've had periods of employment during your working life.

On its own, the basic State Pension is unlikely to provide you with anything like your current standard of living. Therefore, it's crucial that you plan how to provide yourself with the rest of the retirement income you'll need.

An efficient way to save for retirement

One big attraction of being self-employed is that you don't have a boss. But, in terms of pensions, that's a disadvantage.

Workplace schemes can be a convenient way for employees to start contributing to a pension, and in many cases, their employers will contribute too.

If you're self-employed, you won't have an employer adding money to your pension in this way. But you'll still get Income Tax relief on your contributions. If you're a basic-rate taxpayer, for every £100 you pay into your pension, HM Revenue and Customs will add an extra £20.

Start as early as possible

The earlier you start saving into a pension, the better. It gives you more time to contribute to your fund before retirement, more time to benefit from tax relief, and more time for growth in your fund's value due to investment returns and the power of compounded returns.

Starting early could double your pension fund. Someone saving £100 a month for 40 years (say from age 25 until 65) would put the same amount into their pension fund as someone starting 20 years later and putting £200 a month in. However, the early starter would have a much bigger fund on retirement. Assuming 5% investment growth and a product charge of 0.75% throughout the term:

- The person starting at age 25 would build a fund of around £123,000
- The later starter's fund would grow to around £75,000

What kind of pension should you use?

There's a range of different types of pension scheme you can consider, including stakeholder pensions, personal pensions and SIPPs (self-invested personal pensions).

How much can you save?

You can save as much as you like towards your pension each year, but there's a limit on the amount that will get tax relief. The maximum amount of pension savings that benefit from tax relief each year is called the 'annual allowance'. The annual allowance for 2015/16 is £40,000. If you go over £40,000, you won't get tax relief on further pension savings. You can usually carry forward unused annual allowance from the previous three years.

- If your income varies significantly from year to year, unused allowances can allow you to maximise your pension savings in years when your income is high
- You must have been a member of a pension scheme during the years you want to carry forward your unused allowance
- Even with unused annual allowance carried forward, your tax relief is limited by your annual earnings for the year in question
- If you save more than your annual allowance, you may have to pay a tax charge

Pension 'input periods'

Pension payments are made over 12-month periods called 'input periods' – but these don't always follow the tax year and may differ if you pay into different schemes.

- The tax year in which an input period ends determines the annual allowance that is applied
- So, any pension savings for input periods starting before 6 April 2015 but ending in the 2015/16 tax year will count towards the annual allowance limit of £40,000
- Your pension scheme administrator can tell you what your pension input periods are

Options for using your pension pot

You now have more choice and flexibility than ever before.

Following changes introduced in April 2015, you now have more choice and flexibility than ever before over how and when you can take money from your pension pot.

It's important to take your time to understand your options and seek professional financial advice, as what you decide now will affect your retirement income for the rest of your life.

Taking your pension from April 2015

Changes introduced from April 2015 give you freedom over how you can use your pension pot(s), if you're 55 or over and have a pension based on how much has been paid into your pot, a Defined Contribution scheme can provide an income for life for a dependant or other beneficiary after you die.

Use your pot to provide a flexible retirement income – flexi-access drawdown

With this option you take up to 25% of your pension pot or of the amount you allocate for drawdown as a tax-free lump sum, then re-invest the rest into funds designed to provide you with a regular taxable income.

You set the income you want, though this may be adjusted periodically depending on the performance of your investments. Unlike with a lifetime annuity your income isn't guaranteed for life – so you need to manage your investments carefully.

The rest will be taxed at your highest tax rate – by adding it to the rest of your income.

There are many risks associated with cashing in your whole pot. For example, it's highly likely that you'll be landed with a large tax bill – it won't pay you or any dependant a regular income and, without very careful planning, you could run out of money and have nothing to live on in retirement.

Be sure to obtain professional financial advice before cashing in your entire pot.

Option combinations

You don't have to choose one option when deciding how to access your pension – you can opt for a combination and take cash and income at different times to suit your needs. You can also keep saving into a pension if you wish and get tax relief up to age 75.

Annuities

Regular retirement income for life or for a set period

An annuity is a type of retirement income product that you buy with some or all of your pension pot. It pays a regular retirement income either for life or for a set period.

Annuities – the basics

Annuities are retirement income products sold by insurance companies.

They include:

- **Lifetime annuities**–which pay you an income for life, and will pay a nominated beneficiary an income for life after you die if you choose this option; they include basic lifetime annuities and investment-linked annuities

- **Fixed-term annuities**–which pay an income for a set period, usually five or ten years, and then a 'maturity amount' at the end that you can use to buy another retirement income product or take as cash

When you use money from your pension pot to buy an annuity, you can take up to a quarter of the amount as tax-free cash. You then use the rest to buy the annuity and the income you receive is taxed as normal income.

How much retirement income you will get from an annuity – and for how long – will depend on:

- How old you are when you buy your annuity
- How big your pension pot is
- Your health and lifestyle
- Annuity rates at the time you buy

- Which annuity type, income options and features you choose
- Where you expect to live when you retire

Once you buy an annuity you can't change your mind, so it's important to obtain professional financial advice before committing to one.

Higher income for medical conditions or unhealthy lifestyle

If you have a medical condition, are overweight or smoke, you may be able to get a higher income by opting for an 'enhanced' or 'impaired life' annuity. Not all providers offer these so be sure to shop around if you think you might benefit from one.

Your other retirement income options

An annuity is just one of several options you have for using your pension pot to provide a retirement income.

National Employment Savings Trust Pensions

Low-cost option through your workplace

The National Employment Savings Trust (NEST) is a low-cost pension you may be able to join through your workplace or if you are self-employed. Once a member, you can carry on saving this way even if you change jobs or stop working.

What is NEST?

NEST is a pension scheme set up by the Government mainly to help employers with automatic enrolment. Between 2012 and 2018, employers must automatically enrol most of their workers in a workplace pension scheme and pay in contributions on your behalf. Your employer chooses the scheme, but it must meet minimum standards. Many employers are likely to choose NEST.

The main features of NEST are:
- Defined Contribution scheme, so you build up your own pension pot
- Flexible contributions
- Low charges

You can save with NEST if:
- Your current employer enrols you
- A previous employer enrolled you
- You are self-employed
- You are given a share of a NEST pension following divorce or the end of a registered civil partnership

How NEST works

NEST is a Defined Contribution (DC) scheme. This means that the contributions paid in by you, your employer and anyone else are invested and build up your own pension pot. You use this pot to provide yourself with an income in retirement.

Flexible contributions

If you are automatically enrolled into NEST, your employer must contribute, and usually you must pay in a minimum amount too. You can pay in extra if you want to. If you are self-employed, you choose whether to join and how much to save. Tax relief is added to your contributions.

You can stop and start contributions when you like, and pay in regular amounts or single lump sums as long as they are within the NEST limits. The minimum contribution is £10. Total contributions, including those from your employer, must not come to more than a yearly limit, currently £4,700 (2015/16 tax year).

Low charges

NEST has two types of charge:
- A contribution charge set at 1.8% of whatever is paid in. So, if you contribute £10, after the charge £9.82 goes into your pot
- An annual charge of 0.3% of your pension pot. For example, if your pot is worth £1,000 this year, the annual charge will take away £3, leaving £997 invested in the pot for next year

These charges are lower than most personal pensions and much lower than the maximum charges allowed for stakeholder pensions (1.5% annual charge for the first 10 years and 1% a year after that).

Changing jobs

Once you are a member of NEST you can carry on paying in even if you change jobs or stop work. If your new employer offers NEST, then both you and your employer can pay into your existing pension pot.

You cannot transfer any previous pensions you have built up into NEST or transfer your NEST savings to a different scheme.

Self-Invested Personal Pensions (SIPPS)

Providing greater flexibility with the investments you can choose

A self-invested personal pension (SIPP) is a pension 'wrapper' that holds investments until you retire and start to draw a retirement income. It is a type of personal pension and works in a similar way to a standard personal pension. The main difference is that with a SIPP, you have greater flexibility with the investments you can choose.

How it works

With standard personal pension schemes your investments are managed for you within the pooled fund you have chosen. SIPPs are a form of personal pension that give you the freedom to choose and manage your own investments. Another option is to pay an authorised investment manager to make the decisions for you.

SIPPs are designed for people who want to manage their own fund by dealing with and switching their investments when they want to. SIPPs can also have higher charges than other personal pensions or stakeholder pensions. For these reasons SIPPs tend to be more suitable for large funds and for people who are experienced in investing.

What you can and can't invest in

Most SIPPs allow you to select from a range of assets, such as:

- Individual stocks and shares quoted on a recognised UK or overseas stock exchange
- Government securities

- Unit trusts
- Investment trusts
- Insurance company funds
- Traded endowment policies
- Deposit accounts with banks and building societies
- Some National Savings and Investment products
- Commercial property (such as offices, shops or factory premises)

These aren't all of the investment options that are available – different SIPP providers offer different investment options.

Residential property can't be held directly in a SIPP with the tax advantages that usually accompany pension investments. But, subject to some restrictions, personal property can be held in a SIPP through certain types of collective investments, such as real estate investment trusts without losing the tax advantages. Not all SIPP providers accept this type of investment though.

How you access money in your SIPP

New rules introduced in April 2015 mean you can access and use your pension pot in any way you wish from age 55.

SIPPs aren't for everyone, and you should seek professional financial advice if you are considering this option.

Stakeholder Pensions

Minimum standards if you don't want too much choice

Stakeholder pensions are a form of Defined Contribution personal pension. They have low and flexible minimum contributions, capped charges, and a default investment strategy if you don't want too much choice. Some employers offer them but you can start one yourself.

How stakeholder pensions work

Minimum standards

Stakeholder pensions must meet minimum standards set by the Government.

These include:

- Limited charges
- Low minimum contributions
- Flexible contributions
- Charge-free transfers
- A default investment fund – your money will be invested into this if you don't want to choose

While you are working

Your contributions are usually invested in stocks and shares along with other investments, with the aim of growing the fund over the years before you retire. You can usually choose from a range of funds to invest in. Remember though that the value of investments may go up or down.

When you retire

Once you stop working and retire, you can access money in your stakeholder pension.

In fact, you don't have to retire to take money out of your pension as you can do this from the age of 55. There's a lot to weigh up when working out which option or combination will provide you and any dependants with a reliable and tax-efficient income throughout your retirement.

Setting up a stakeholder pension

If a stakeholder pension is offered through your employer it will have chosen the pension provider and may also arrange for contributions to be paid from your wages or salary. The employer may contribute to the scheme.

The pension provider claims tax relief at the basic rate and adds it to your fund. If you are a higher or additional-rate taxpayer you'll need to claim the additional rebate through your tax return.

You can also set up a stakeholder pension for yourself. Their flexibility, low minimum contributions and capped charges can be of particular benefit if you're self-employed or on a low income.

Changing jobs

If you change jobs, you should check to see if your new employer offers a pension scheme. You can continue paying into an existing stakeholder pension, but you may find you'll be better off joining your new employer's scheme, especially if the employer contributes. Compare the benefits available through your employer's scheme with your stakeholder pension.

If you decide to stop paying into a stakeholder pension you can leave the pension fund to carry on growing, mainly through investment growth, but check to see if there are extra charges for doing this.

Defined Benefit Pension Schemes

A secure income for life

A Defined Benefit (DB) pension scheme is one where the amount paid to you is set using a formula based on how many years you've worked for your employer and the salary you've earned rather than the value of your investments. If you work or have worked for a large employer or in the public sector, you may have a DB pension.

How Defined Benefit pensions work

Defined Benefit (DB) pensions pay out a secure income for life which increases each year. They also usually pay a pension to your spouse or registered civil partner and/or your dependants when you die.

The pension income they pay is based on:
- The number of years you've been a member of the scheme – known as 'pensionable service'
- Your pensionable earnings – this could be your salary at retirement (known as 'final salary'), or salary averaged over a career ('career average'), or some other formula
- The proportion of those earnings you receive as a pension for each year of membership – this is called the 'accrual rate', and some commonly used rates are 1/60th or 1/80th of your pensionable earnings for each year of pensionable service

These schemes are run by trustees who look after the interests of the scheme's members. Your employer contributes to the scheme and is responsible for ensuring there is enough money at the time you retire to pay your pension income.

How much will my income be?

Check your latest pension statement to get an idea of how much your pension income may be. Statements vary from one scheme to another but they usually show your age. Contact your pension administrator if you're not receiving your annual statement.

When you take your pension, you can usually choose to take up to 25% of the value of your pension as a tax-free lump sum.

With most schemes, your pension income is reduced if you take this tax-free cash. The more you take, the lower your income. However, some schemes, particularly public sector pension schemes, pay a tax-free lump sum automatically and in addition to the pension income.

Make sure you understand whether the pension shown on your statement is the amount you'll get before or after taking a tax-free lump sum.

Also, don't forget that your actual pension based on your current salary, how long you've been in the scheme and pension income will be taxable.

Find our what your pension might be if you stay in the scheme until the scheme's normal retirement age (usually 65).

If your scheme allows, you may be able to take your pension earlier (from the age of 55) but this can reduce the amount you get quite considerably. It's possible to take your pension without retiring.

Again, depending on your scheme you may be able to defer taking your pension, and this might mean you get a higher income when you do take it. Check with your scheme for details.

Once you pension starts to be paid, it will increase each year by a set amount - your scheme rules will tell you by how much. It will continue to be paid for life. When you die, a pension may continue to be paid to your spouse, civil partner and/or dependants. This is usually a fixed percentage (for example, 50%) of your pension income at the date of your death.

Taking your pension as a lump sum

You may be able to take your whole pension as a cash lump sum. If you do this, up to 25% of the sum will be tax-free and the rest will be subject to Income Tax.

You can do this from age 55 (or earlier if you're seriously ill) and in the following circumstances:

- You can take the whole of your pension as cash if the total value of all your pension savings is less than £30,000
- You can take your pension as cash if it's worth less than £10,000, regardless of how much your other pension savings are. You can do this for up to three different pensions

Transferring your Defined Benefit pension

If you're in a private sector DB pension scheme or a funded public sector scheme, you can transfer to a Defined Contribution (DC) pension as long as you're not already taking your pension.

DC pensions can be accessed flexibly from age 55, so this may seem like an attractive option.

However, in most cases, you may be worse off in a DC pension and for this reason it's rarely a good idea to transfer even if your employer offers incentives for you to switch.

If you're in an unfunded DB pension scheme (these are mainly public sector pension schemes), you will not be able to transfer to a DC pension scheme but will still be able to transfer to another DB pension scheme.

Protection for your Defined Benefit pension

The Pension Protection Fund protects DB schemes. This pays some compensation to scheme members whose employers become insolvent and where the scheme doesn't have enough funds to pay members' benefits. The compensation may not be the full amount as the level of protection varies between members already drawing benefits, those who are still contributing to the scheme and deferred members who have left the scheme but have built up an entitlement.

Personal Pensions

A good way of saving for retirement

A personal pension is a type of Defined Contribution (DC) pension. You choose the provider and make arrangements for your contributions to be paid. If you don't have a workplace pension, getting a personal pension could be a good way of saving for retirement.

Tax relief

Your pension provider will claim tax relief at the basic rate and add it to your pension pot. If you're a higher-rate taxpayer you'll need to claim the additional rebate through your tax return. You also choose where you want your contributions to be invested from a range of funds offered by your provider.

How they work

Your pension pot builds up in line with the contributions you make, investment returns and tax relief.

You can usually choose from a range of funds to invest in. Remember that the value of investments may go up or down.

When you retire the size of your pension pot will depend on:

- How much you pay into your pension pot
- How long you save for
- How much, if anything, your employer pays in
- How well your investments have performed
- What charges have been taken out of your pot by your pension provider

Following changes introduced in April 2015, you now have more choice and employers offer to their workers. As with other types of DC scheme, members in a GPP build up a personal pension pot which they then convert into an income at retirement.

Changing jobs

If you change jobs check when your new employer will enrol you into a workplace pension scheme.

You can continue paying into an existing personal pension, but you may find you'll be better off joining your employer's workplace pension scheme, especially if your employer contributes. Compare the benefits available through your employer's scheme with your personal pension.

RELIEF ON PENSION CONTRIBUTIONS
Annual and lifetime limits to consider

Tax relief means some of your money that would have gone to the Government as tax goes into your pension instead. You can put as much as you want into your pension, but there are annual and lifetime limits on how much tax relief you get on your pension contributions.

Tax relief on your annual pension contributions

- If you're a UK taxpayer, in the tax year 2015/16 the standard rule is that you'll get tax relief on pension contributions of up to 100% of your earnings or a £40,000 annual allowance, whichever is lower.
- For example, if you earn £20,000 but put £25,000 into your pension pot (perhaps by topping up earnings with some savings), you'll only get tax relief on £20,000
- Similarly, if you earn £60,000 and want to put that amount in your pension scheme in a single year, you'll only get tax relief on £40,000

Any contributions you make over this limit will be subject to Income Tax at the highest rate you pay.

You can carry forward unused allowances from the previous three years, as long as you were a member of a pension scheme during those years. However, there is an exception to this standard rule. If you have a Defined Contribution pension, the annual allowance reduces to £10,000 in some situations.

From April 2016, the £40,000 annual allowance will be reduced if you have an income of over £150,000, including pension contributions.

The Money Purchase Annual Allowance (MPAA)

In the tax year 2015/16, if you start to take money from your Defined Contribution pension, this can trigger a lower annual allowance of £10,000 (the MPAA). That means you'll only receive tax relief on pension contributions of up to 100% of your earnings or £10,000, whichever is lower.

Whether the new lower £10,000 annual allowance applies depends on how you access your pension pot, and there are some complicated rules around this.

As a basic guide, the main situations when you'll trigger the MPAA are:

- If you start to take ad-hoc lump sums from your pension pot
- If you put your pension pot money into an income drawdown fund and start to take income

In addition, you won't trigger it if you take:

- A tax-free cash lump sum and buy an annuity (an insurance product that gives you a guaranteed income for life)
- A tax-free cash lump sum and put your pension pot into an income drawdown product but don't take any income from it.

You can't carry over any unused MPAA to another tax year.

The lower annual allowance of £10,000 only applies to contributions to Defined Contribution pensions.

So, if you also have a Defined Benefit pension (this pays a retirement income based on your final salary and how long you have worked for your employer and includes final salary and career average pension schemes), you can still receive tax relief on up to £40,000 of contributions a year.

Tax relief if you're a non-taxpayer

If you are not earning enough to pay Income Tax, you can still receive tax relief on pension contributions up to a maximum of £3,600 a year or 100% of earnings, whichever is greater, subject to your annual allowance. For example, if you have relevant income below £3,600, the maximum you can pay in is £2,880 and the Government will top up your contribution to make it £3,600.

How much can you build up in your pension?

A lifetime allowance puts a top limit on the value of pension benefits that you can receive without having to pay a tax charge. The lifetime allowance is £1.25 million for the tax year 2015/16 (falling to £1 million in April 2016).

Any amount above this is subject to a tax charge of 25% if paid as pension or 55% if paid as a lump sum.

Workplace pensions, automatic enrolment and tax relief

Since October 2012, a system is being gradually phased in requiring employers to automatically enrol all eligible workers into a workplace pension.

It requires a minimum total contribution, made up of the employer's contribution, the worker's contribution and the tax relief.

Defined Contribution Pension Schemes

Providing an income in retirement

With a Defined Contribution (DC) pension, you build up a pot of money that you can then use to provide an income in retirement. Unlike Defined Benefit schemes, which promise a specific income, the income you might get from a DC scheme depends on factors including the amount you pay in, the fund's investment performance and the choices you make at retirement.

What is a Defined Contribution pension?

DC pensions build up a pension pot using your contributions and your employer's contributions (if applicable) plus investment returns and tax relief.

If you're a member of the scheme through your workplace, then your employer usually deducts your contributions from your salary before it is taxed. If you've set the scheme up for yourself, you arrange the contributions yourself.

While you are working

The fund is usually invested in stocks and shares, along with other investments, with the aim of growing it over the years before you retire. You can usually choose from a range of funds to invest in. Remember though that the value of investments can go up or down.

When you retire

You can access and use your pension pot in any way you wish from age 55.

You can:

- Take your whole pension pot as a lump sum in one go. 25% will be tax-free and the rest will be subject to Income Tax and taxed in the usual way. Bear in mind that a large lump sum could tip you into a higher tax bracket for the year.
- Take lump sums as and when you need them. A quarter of each lump sum will be tax-free and the rest will be subject to Income Tax and taxed in the usual way. Bear in mind that a large lump sum could tip you into a higher tax bracket for the year.
- Take a quarter of your pension pot (or of the amount you allocate for drawdown) as a tax-free lump sum, then use the rest to provide a regular taxable income.
- Take a quarter of your pot as a tax- free lump sum and then convert some or all of the rest into a taxable retirement income (known as an 'annuity').

The size of your pension pot and amount of income you get when you retire will depend on:
- How much you pay into your pot
- How long you save for
- How much your employer pays in (if a workplace pension)
- How well your investments have performed
- What charges have been taken out of your pot by your pension provider
- How much you take as a cash lump sum
- The choices you make when you retire
- Annuity rates at the time you retire – if you choose the annuity route

When you retire, your pension provider will usually offer you a retirement income (an annuity) based on your pot size, but you don't have to take this and it isn't your only option.

What you need to think about

If your work gives you access to a pension that your employer will pay into, staying out is like turning down the offer of a pay rise. The amount your employer puts in can depend on how much you're willing to save, and may increase as you get older.

Lifetime Annuities

Guaranteeing a regular retirement income for life

A lifetime annuity is a type of retirement income product that you buy with some or all of your pension pot. It guarantees a regular retirement income for life. Lifetime annuity options and features vary – what is suitable for you will depend on your personal circumstances, your life expectancy and your attitude to risk.

How a lifetime annuity works

You choose to take up to 25% of your pension pot – or of the amount you are allocating to buy an annuity –as a tax- free lump sum. You then use the rest to buy an annuity, which will provide you with a regular income for life.

This retirement income is taxed as normal income. As a rule of thumb, the older you are when you take out an annuity, the higher the income (annuity rate) you'll get.

There are two types of lifetime annuity to choose from:

- **Basic lifetime annuities**–where you set your income in advance
- **Investment-linked annuities**–where your income rises and falls in line with investment performance, but will never fall below a guaranteed minimum

Basic lifetime annuities

Basic lifetime annuities offer a range of income options designed to match different personal circumstances and attitude to risk.

You need to decide whether you want:

- One that provides an income for life for you only – a single life annuity, or one that also provides an income for life for a dependant or other nominated beneficiary after you die – called a 'joint-life annuity'
- Payments to continue to a nominated beneficiary for a set number of years (for example, 10 years) from the time the annuity starts in case you die unexpectedly early – called a 'guarantee period'
- 'Value protection'–less commonly used, but designed to pay your nominated beneficiary the value of the pot used to buy the annuity less income already paid out when you die
- Your choices affect how much income you can get, and where you expect to live when you retire may also affect how much income you get.

Higher income for medical conditions or unhealthy lifestyle

If you have a medical condition, are overweight or smoke, you may be able to get a higher income by opting for an 'enhanced' or impaired life' annuity.

Not all providers offer these so be sure to shop around if you think you might benefit from one.

Remember, a lifetime annuity is just one of several options you have for taking a retirement income.

Investment-linked Annuities

Values dependent on how well the underlying investments perform. Investment-linked annuities also pay you an income for life, but the amount you get fluctuates depending on how well the underlying investments perform. If the investments do well, they offer the chance of a higher income. But you have to be comfortable with the risk that your income could fall if the investments don't do as well as expected.

All investment-linked annuities guarantee a minimum income if the fund's performance is weak.

With investment-linked annuities, you can also opt for joint or single annuity, guarantee periods, value protection and higher rates if you have a short life expectancy due to poor health or lifestyle. An annuity may not be the right option for you. Think carefully about whether you need to provide an income for your partner or another dependant after you die.

What happens when you die?

If you have a single annuity and no other features, your pension stops when you die. Otherwise, the tax rules vary depending on your age.

If you die before age 75, any income from a joint annuity will be paid to your dependant or other nominated beneficiary tax-free for the rest of their life.

If you die within a guarantee period, the remaining annuity payments will pass tax- free to your nominated beneficiary then stop when the guarantee period ends. Any lump sum payment due from a value-protected annuity will be paid tax-free.

Other things to note:
- Joint annuity payments will stop when your dependant or other beneficiary dies
- Any guarantee period payments stop when the guarantee period ends
- Any lump sum due from a value protected annuity will be taxable at 45% if paid before 6 April 2016 and at the beneficiary's highest tax rate if paid after that

Flexi-access drawdown

Using your pension pot for a flexible retirement income

With flexi-access drawdown when you come to take your pension you reinvest your pot into funds designed to provide you with a regular retirement income. This income may vary depending on the fund's performance and it isn't guaranteed for life.

How flexi-access drawdown works

You can choose to take up to 25% of your pension pot as a tax-free lump sum. You then move the rest into one or more funds that allow you to take a taxable income at times to suit you. Most people will use it to take a regular income.

You choose funds to invest in that match your income objectives and attitude to risk and set the income you want. The income you receive may be adjusted periodically depending on the performance of your investments.

Once you've taken your tax-free lump sum, you can start taking the income right away or wait until a later date.

You can also move your pension pot gradually into income drawdown. You can take up to a quarter of each amount you move from your pot tax-free and place the rest into income drawdown.

Using drawdown funds for other products

To help provide more certainty, you can at any time use all or part of the funds in your income drawdown to buy an annuity or other type of retirement income product that may offer guarantees about growth and/or income. What's available in the market will vary at any given time so you'll need to obtain professional financial advice.

Things to think about

You need to carefully plan how much income you can afford to take under flexi-access drawdown otherwise there's a risk you'll run out of money.

This could happen if:
- You take out too much in the early years
- Your investments don't perform as well as you expect and you don't adjust the amount you take accordingly
- You live longer than you've planned for

If you choose flexi-access drawdown, it's important to regularly review your investments. Unless you're an experienced investor you may well need professional financial advice to help with this.

Not all pension schemes or providers offer flexi-access drawdown. Even if yours does it's important to compare what else is on the market as charges, the choice of funds and flexibility may vary from one provider to another.

What tax will I pay?

Any money you take from your pension pot using income drawdown will be added to your income for the year and taxed in the normal way. Large withdrawals could push you into a higher tax band so bear this in mind when deciding how much to take and when.

If the value of all of your pension savings is above £1.25m when you access your pot (2015/16 tax year), further tax charges may apply.

Tax relief on future pension saving

If the value of your pension pot is £10,000 or more, once you start to take income, the amount of Defined Contribution pension savings which you can get tax relief on each year falls rom £40,000 (the 'annual allowance') to £10,000 (called the 'Money Purchase Annual Allowance' or MPAA). If you want to carry on building up your pension pot, this may influence when you start aking income.

What happens when you die?

You can nominate who you'd like to receive any money left in your drawdown fund when you die.

If you die before the age of 75, any money left in your drawdown und passes tax-free to your nominated beneficiary whether they ake it as a lump sum or as income. These payments must begin within two years, or the beneficiary will have to pay income tax on hem

If you die after the age of 75 and your nominated beneficiary akes the money as income, they will pay tax on it in the normal way. f they take the money as a lump sum before 6 April 2016, they'll pay 45% tax on it – any lump sum taken on or after this date will be added o their income and taxed in the normal way

Is flexi-access drawdown right for me?

ncome drawdown is a complex product, and you should seek professional financial advice to assess whether it is suitable for you. Flexi-access drawdown is just one of several options you have for using your pension pot to provide a retirement income.

Taking Small Cash Sums From Your Pension Pot

Consider the tax implications and the risk that your money could run out

Under new flexible rules introduced in April 2015, you can now use your pension pot to take out cash as and when you need it. However, there are tax implications and a risk that your money could run out.

How it works

You take cash from your pension pot whenever you need it. For each cash withdrawal, the first 25% will be tax-free and the rest will be taxed at your highest tax rate by adding it to the rest of your income. There may be charges each time you make a cash withdrawal and/or limits on how many withdrawals you can make each year.

Unlike with the option called flexi-access drawdown, your pension pot isn't reinvested into funds that are actively managed to pay a regular income – this means there's more risk that its value could fall.

Things to think about
- Your pension pot reduces with each cash withdrawal. The earlier you start taking money out of your pot, the greater the risk your money could run out. What's left in your pension pot might not grow enough to give you the income you need to last you into old age – most people underestimate how long their retirement will be.
- The administration charges for each withdrawal could eat into your remaining pot. The funds where your existing pot is invested could fall in value and you could run out of money.

- Because your pot hasn't been reinvested to produce an income, its investments could fall in value – so you'll need to have it reviewed regularly. Charges will apply and you may need to move or reinvest your pot at a later date.
- Once you take money out of your pension pot, any growth in its value is taxable, whereas it will grow tax-free inside the pot – once you take it out, you can't put it back.
- Taking cash lump sums could also reduce your entitlement to benefits now or as you grow older.

Tax you will pay

Three quarters of each cash withdrawal counts as taxable income. This is added to the rest of your income, and depending on how much your total income for the tax year is you could find yourself pushed into a higher tax band. Therefore, if you take lots of large cash sums, or even a single cash sum, you could end up paying a higher rate of tax than you normally do.

Your pension scheme or provider will pay the cash through a payslip and take off tax in advance – called 'PAYE' (Pay As You Earn). This means you may pay too much tax and have to claim the money back – or you may owe more tax if you have other sources of income.

Extra tax charges or restrictions may apply if your pension savings exceed the lifetime allowance (currently £1.25m), or if you have less lifetime allowance available than the amount you want to withdraw.

Tax relief on future pension savings

If the value of your pension pot is £10,000 or more, once you start to take income the amount of Defined Contribution pension savings on which you can get tax relief each year is reduced from £40,000 (the 'annual allowance') to £10,000 (called the 'Money Purchase annual Allowance' or 'MPAA'). If you want to carry on building up your pension pot this option may not be suitable.

What happens when you die?
- If you die before the age of 75, any untouched part of your pension pot will pass tax-free to your nominated beneficiary or estate
- If you die after the age of 75 or over and your nominated beneficiary takes the money as income, they will pay tax on it in the normal way. If they take the money as a lump sum **before 6 April 2016**, they'll pay 45% tax on it – any lump sum taken on or after this date will be added to their income and taxed in the normal way

The lifetime allowance charge

If the value of all of your pension savings is above £1.25m when you die, further tax charges may apply.

Your other retirement income options

Taking cash sums is just one of several options you have for using your pension pot to provide a retirement income. Because of the risk of running out of money, we don't recommend using this method to fund your retirement income.

Taking Your Whole Pension Pot As Cash

A high-risk and non-tax-efficient way to fund your retirement income

Under new rules introduced in April 2015, you can now take the whole of your pension pot as cash in one go if you wish. However, if you do this you could end up with a large tax bill and run out of money in retirement.

How it works

To take your whole pension pot as cash you simply close your pension pot and withdraw it all. The first 25% will be tax-free, the remaining 75% will be taxed at your highest tax rate – by adding it to the rest of your income.

Things to think about

Help with long-term care needs, and not all pension schemes and providers offer the facility to withdraw cash – if yours doesn't shop around as charges will vary, but get guidance or advice before you commit.

You may not be able to use this option if you have received a share of an ex- spouse or ex-civil partner's pension as a result of a divorce, or if you have certain protected rights with your pension. Check with your scheme or provider.

Tax you will pay

Remember, 75% of the amount you withdraw counts as taxable income. It is highly likely this will increase your tax rate when added to your other income. Your pension scheme or provider will pay the cash through a payslip and take off tax in advance – called 'PAYE' (Pay As You Earn).

This means you may pay too much Income Tax and have to claim the money back – or you may owe more tax if you have other sources of income available than the value of the pension pot you want to cash in.

Tax relief on future pension savings

If the value of the pension pot you cash in is £10,000 or more, once you have taken the cash the annual amount of Defined Contribution pension savings on which you can get tax relief is reduced from £40,000 (the Money Purchase Annual Allowance or MPAA) to £10,000 (MPAA). If you want to carry on building up your pension pot this option may not be suitable.

Lifetime Allowance for Pension Savings

Limiting the value of pay-outs from pension schemes

The lifetime allowance is a limit on the value of payouts from your pension schemes – whether lump sums or retirement income – that can be made without triggering an extra tax charge.

How much is the lifetime allowance?

The lifetime allowance for most people is £1.25 million in the tax year 2015/16 (reduced from £1.5 million in 2013/14 and falling to £1 million from 6 April 2016). It applies to the total of all the pensions you have, including the value of pensions promised through any Defined Benefit schemes you belong to, but excluding your State Pension.

Protecting your lifetime allowance

If your total pension savings exceed £1.25 million you may be able to apply for protection – called 'Individual Protection 2014'.

Level of protection

Completing HM Revenue & Customs (HMRC) form IP2014 will give you a protected lifetime allowance equal to the value of your pension savings on 5 April 2014 subject to an overall maximum of £1.5 million.

Can you continue saving into a pension?

Yes, you can continue saving into a pension but any pension savings above the protected lifetime allowance will be liable for tax on the excess called the 'lifetime allowance charge'.

How to apply

There is a three-year period in which you can apply for IP2014 (6 April 2014 to 5 April 2017). You will have up to 5 April 2017 to submit your IP2014 application to HMRC.

Contribution or a Defined Benefit pension scheme.

Working out if this applies to you

Every time a pay out from your pension scheme starts, its value is compared against your remaining lifetime allowance to see if there is additional tax to pay.

You can work out whether you are likely to be affected by adding up the expected value of your payouts.

You work out the value of pensions differently depending on the type of scheme you are in:

- For defined contribution pension schemes, including all personal pensions, the value of your benefits will be the value of your pension pot used to fund your retirement income and any lump sum
- For defined benefit pension schemes, you calculate the total value by multiplying your expected annual pension by 20. In addition, you need to add to this the amount of any tax- free cash lump sum if it is additional to the pension. In many schemes, you would only get a lump sum by giving up some of your pension, in which case the value of the full pension captures the full value of your payouts. So you are likely to be affected by the lifetime allowance in 2015/2016 if you are on track for a final salary pension (with no separate lump sum) of more than £62,500 a year or a salary-related pension over £46,875, plus the maximum tax-free cash lump sum

Note that certain tax-free lump sum benefits paid out to your survivors if you die before age 75 also use up lifetime allowance

For example, suppose someone who pays tax at the higher rate had expected to get £1,000 a year as income but the 25% lifetime allowance reduced this to £750 a year. After Income Tax at 40%, the person would be left with £450 a year.

This means the lifetime allowance charge and Income Tax combined have reduced the income by 55% – the same as the lifetime allowance charge had the benefits been taken as a lump sum instead of income.

Think carefully before continuing as an active member of a Defined Benefits scheme – opting out of active membership and becoming a deferred member significantly reduces the risk of losing your protection.

Chapter 11

Few taxes are quite as emotive – or as politicised – as Inheritance Tax

Few taxes are quite as emotive – or as politicised – as Inheritance Tax (IHT). The structures into which you transfer your assets can have lasting consequences for you and your family. We can help you choose structures and trusts designed to protect your assets and give your family lasting benefits.

Historically, IHT planning used to be an activity confined to the very rich. However, growing affluence means that this is no longer the case. Even families and individuals with a relatively moderate level of wealth should consider planning ahead to ensure that their assets are passed on to their loved ones as efficiently as possible.

Property price increases have dragged many middle-class working families into the IHT bracket. The Office for Budget Responsibility (OBR) calculates that 4.8% of the population currently pays IHT. By 2018/19, it estimates that figure will have more than doubled to 10%. Many argue that the threshold should at least rise each year in line with inflation, but now the rate has been fixed since 2009.

Effective estate planning is about getting the right balance between maintaining access to your money when you need it and saving tax. This is because in general, the more tax-efficient a solution is, the less access you have to your assets. Safeguarding your own financial future is very important, and giving too much away could put this at risk.

The best way to avoid paying any IHT is to reduce your estate value to below the current £325,000 IHT threshold, but this is not practical for many people. New changes to pension legislation could also offer a way around IHT.

From 6 April 2015, pension pots are now no longer subject to a 55% tax when passed on to loved ones after the saver dies. This means that any funds in a pension pot can be passed on to a named individual without any tax implications if they die before the age of 75. In some situations, it may be appropriate to consider transferring all your non-pension assets to fund your pension. By shifting your savings into a drawdown scheme they will no longer be included in your final estate valuation, and therefore will avoid Inheritance Tax.

This is a very complex area of financial planning and despite all the options available, unless you give your home away, it may be difficult to avoid IHT on what is probably your most valuable asset.

Protecting and preserving your wealth

One thing is certain: you should obtain professional financial advice if you have any concerns about how to mitigate IHT. To find out more about our services, or to discuss how we could help you to protect and preserve your wealth, please contact us. We look forward to hearing from you.

Content of the articles featured is for general information and use only and is not intended to address an individual or company's particular requirements or be deemed to be, or constitute, advice. Although endeavours have been made to provide accurate and timely information, there can be no guarantee that such information is accurate as of the date it is received or that it will continue to be accurate in the future.

No individual or company should act upon such information without receiving appropriate professional advice after a thorough examination of their particular situation.

We cannot accept responsibility for any loss as a result of acts or omissions taken in respect of any articles. Thresholds, percentage rates and tax legislation may change in subsequent Finance Acts.

HISTORY LESSON

Inheritance Tax matters

Inheritance Tax was introduced in the UK in 1796 and stemmed from the influence of the French Revolution. The concept of IHT was supposed to protect poorer members of society and interrupt the legacy of inherited wealth.

When the tax was first introduced, it was known as 'legacy, estate and succession duties' and was collected on properties worth over a certain value. By 1857, this value had settled at £20, but duties were rarely collected on properties under £1,500. The duties evolved into death duties in 1894 and did have a significant role to play in breaking up large estates in the UK. In this sense then, the original aim of the tax yielded some results.

Allowance without special tax planning

In 2010, further changes to IHT were made, increasing the nil-rate threshold to come into line with rising house prices.

IHT is paid if a person's estate (their property, money and possessions) is currently worth more than £325,000 when they die. It doubles to £650,000 for a married couple or registered civil partnership – as long as the first person to die leaves their entire estate to their partner. This is called the 'Inheritance Tax threshold'.

The rate of Inheritance Tax is 40% on anything above the threshold. The rate may be reduced to 36% if 10% or more of the estate is left to charity.

PREVENTATIVE ACTION TAKING

Reducing your beneficiaries' potential Inheritance Tax bill – or mitigating it out altogether

With careful planning and professional financial advice, it is possible to take preventative action to either reduce your beneficiaries' potential Inheritance Tax bill or mitigate it out altogether.

1. Make a Will

A vital element of effective estate planning is to make a Will – unfortunately, a significant number of adults with children under 18 fail to do so. This is mainly due to apathy, but also a result of the fact that many of us are uncomfortable talking about issues surrounding our death. Making a Will ensures your assets are distributed in accordance with your wishes.

This is particularly important if you have a spouse or partner, as there is no IHT payable between the two of you, but there could be tax payable if you die intestate – without a Will – and assets end up going to other relatives.

2. Make allowable gifts

You can give cash or gifts worth up to £3,000 in total each tax year, and these will be exempt from Inheritance Tax when you die.

You can carry forward any unused part of the £3,000 exemption to the following year, but then you must use it or lose it.

Parents can give cash or gifts worth up to £5,000 when a child gets married, grandparents up to £2,500 and anyone else up to £1,000. Small gifts of up to £250 a year can also be made to as many people as you like.

3. Give away assets

Parents are increasingly providing children with funds to help them buy their own home. This can be done through a gift and, provided the parents survive for seven years after making it, the money automatically ends up outside their estate for IHT calculations – irrespective of size.

4. Make use of trusts

Assets can be put in trust, thereby no longer forming part of the estate. There are many types of trust available, and they usually involve parents (called 'settlors') investing a sum of money into a trust.

The trust has to be set up with trustees – a suggested minimum of two – whose role is to ensure that on the death of the settlors, the investment is paid out according to the settlors' wishes. In most cases, this will be to children or grandchildren.

The most widely used trust is a 'discretionary' trust, which can be set up in a way that the settlors (parents) still have access to income or parts of the capital.

It can seem daunting to put money away in a trust, but they can be unwound in the event of a family crisis and monies returned to the settlors via the beneficiaries.

5. The income over expenditure rule

As well as putting lump sums into a trust, you can also make monthly contributions.

Paying Inheritance Tax

Estimating how much liability you could leave behind for your loved ones

Usually the 'executor' of the Will or the 'administrator' of the estate pays Inheritance Tax using funds from the estate.

An executor is a person named in the Will to deal with the estate – there can be more than one. An administrator is the person who deals with the estate if there's no Will; Trustees are responsible for paying IHT on trusts.

Married couples and registered civil partners are allowed to pass their possessions and assets to each other tax-free and since October 2007, the surviving partner is now allowed to use both tax-free allowances (providing one wasn't used at the first death).

Gifts made within the last seven years are not included in the calculations but may be liable to IHT on a sliding scale.

The calculation for valuation of your estate is for your general information and use only and is not intended to address your particular requirements. It should not be relied upon in its entirety and shall not be deemed to be, or constitute, advice.

No individual or company should act upon such information without receiving appropriate professional advice after a thorough examination of their particular situation.

If IHT is due on the estate, you would need to complete HM Revenue & Customs (HMRC) form IHT400. You may also need to send other forms at the same time.

If no IHT is due, you'll need to complete form IHT205 to tell HMRC that no IHT is due on the estate.

You or your solicitor will need to send the forms with your application for probate ('grant of representation'). This is called 'confirmation' in Scotland.

The grant of representation (confirmation) gives you the right to deal with the estate as the executor or administrator.

Deadline for paying Inheritance Tax

The executor of a Will or administrator of an estate usually has to pay IHT by the end of the sixth month after the person died. After this, the estate has to pay interest.

Gifts

Small gifts that don't create an Inheritance Tax liability

HM Revenue & Customs allows you to make a number of small gifts each year without creating an Inheritance Tax liability. Remember, each person has their own allowance so the amount can be doubled if each spouse or registered civil partner uses their allowances.

You can also make larger gifts, but these are known as 'Potentially Exempt Transfers' (PETs), and you could have to pay IHT on their value if you die within seven years of making them.

The estate may not have to pay IHT on assets the deceased gave away as gifts while they were alive.

A gift can be:
- Anything that has a value, for example, money, property or possessions
- A loss in value when somethings transferred, for example, if a parent sells a house to a child for less than it's worth, the difference in value counts as a gift

- There's no IHT payable on any gift married couples or registered civil partners give each other – as long as they live in the UK permanently

Seven-year rule

Taper relief applies where tax, or additional tax, becomes payable on your death in respect of gifts made during your lifetime. The relief works on a sliding scale.

The relief is given against the amount of tax you'd have to pay rather than the value of the gift itself. The value of the gift is set when it's given, not at the time of death.

The original owner must live for seven years after giving the gift. If they don't, their estate or the person who received it will have to pay IHT on it.

The amount due is reduced on a sliding scale if the gift was given away between three and seven years before the person died.

For example:
- You'd made a non-exempt gift of £350,000 on 1 February 2011 and died on 20 June 2014
- The IHT nil rate threshold at the date of death was £325,000 the next, but the maximum exemption is £6,000.

Certain gifts don't count towards the annual exemption and no IHT is due on them, for example, wedding gifts and individual gifts worth up to £250.

Wedding gifts

There's no IHT on a gift that was a wedding or registered civil partnership gift worth up to:
- £5,000 to a child
- £2,500 to a grandchild or great-grandchild
- £1,000 to anyone else

The gift must be given on or shortly before the date of the wedding or registered civil partnership ceremony.

Gifts up to £250

There's no IHT payable on individual gifts worth up to £250 – unless in the same tax year, the deceased gave the same person:
- More than £250 worth of gifts
- Other gifts that are free from Inheritance Tax, for example, a wedding gift or a gift that counts towards their £3,000 annual exemption
- Regular gifts from the giver's income

There's no IHT payable on gifts from the deceased's income (after they paid tax) as long as the deceased had enough money to maintain their normal lifestyle. The gifts include:
- Christmas, birthday and wedding or registered civil partnership anniversary presents
- Life insurance policy premiums
- Regular payments into a savings account
- Payments to help with living costs

There's no IHT payable on gifts to help with other people's living costs. These include payments to:
- An ex-husband, ex-wife or former registered civil partner
- A relative who's dependent on them because of old age, illness or disability
- A child (including adopted and stepchild) under 18 years old or in full- time education

Charities

There's no IHT payable on gifts to charities, museums, universities or community amateur sports clubs.

Political parties

There's no IHT payable on gifts to political parties that have either:

- Two members elected to the House of Commons
- One member elected to the House of Commons and received at least 150,000 votes in a general election

Taper relief applies where tax, or additional tax, becomes payable on your death in respect of gifts made during your lifetime.

WHAT A RELIEF

Assets that pass on free of Inheritance Tax

Inheritance Tax reliefs allow some assets to be passed on free of IHT or with a reduced bill.

The executor of a Will or administrator of an estate should claim the reliefs when they're working out how much the estate is worth.

Business Relief

Business Relief allows a business to be passed on as a going concern by reducing the IHT on it by up to 100%.

Agricultural Relief

Agricultural Relief allows a working farm to be passed on as a going concern without paying IHT on it.

Woodland Relief

You don't include the value of the timber in a woodland when you're working out the value of an estate but must include the value of the land.

Whoever inherits the woodland may have to pay IHT when they sell the timber – unless it qualifies for Agricultural or

Business Relief. If the woodland also qualifies for Agricultural Relief or Business Relief (for example, if it's part of a working farm or business), it won't qualify for Woodland Relief.

Heritage assets

Some buildings, land and works of art that have historic or scientific interest may be exempt from IHT.

The assets must be made available for the public to view and meet other conditions to qualify as exempt.

Heritage assets can also be transferred to the Crown to pay an IHT bill.

Passing on a home

How much IHT is charged on a home depends on how the person who died owned it and how they passed it on.

Passing on a home as a gift

If a person passed on their home to their children (or someone else) before they died, it's treated as a gift and the seven-year rule applies.

However, if they continued to live in it rent free, their estate has to pay Inheritance Tax on the home even if they lived for seven years after giving it away. This is known as a 'gift with reservation of benefit'.

Giving away the home and moving out

The original owner can make social visits and stay for short periods in a home they've given away without affecting the seven-year rule.

Giving away part of the home to someone who moves in

If a person gave away half their home to their children (or someone else), who moved in and shared the bills, the half given away won't be included in the valuation of the estate.

Giving away the home and living in it

If the original owner lives in the home after giving it away, they must pay the new owner a 'market rent' (the going rate for similar local rental properties).

Selling a home and giving away the money

If someone sold their home and gave the money to their children (or someone else), the money will be treated as a gift and the seven-year rule will apply.

Leaving assets to a spouse or registered civil partner

An estate is exempt from IHT if the deceased left everything to their husband, wife or registered civil partner who lives permanently in the UK.

The executor or administrator of the estate should give the surviving husband, wife or registered civil partner documents that show any unused IHT threshold. These will be needed to transfer the threshold to the surviving partner's estate when they die.

GIVING TO CHARITY

Reducing an Inheritance Tax – it's good to give

An estate can pay Inheritance Tax at a reduced rate of 36% on some assets (instead of 40%) if 10% or more of the 'net value' of their estate is left to charity.

The net value of an estate is the total value of all the assets after deducting:
- Debts and liabilities & Reliefs

Exemptions

For example:
- Anything left to a husband, wife or civil partner
- Anything below the IHT threshold of £325,000 (the nil rate band)
- An estate doesn't have to pay IHT on any gifts given to charities, museums, universities or community amateur sports clubs.

Which charities you can leave assets to, to pay the reduced rate, the assets must be left to:

- Charities with an HM Revenue and Customs (HMRC) charity reference number
- Community amateur sports clubs (CASCs)

Writing a Will

You can write a clause into your Will to make sure that you'll leave 10% of your estate to charity.

Change a Will

The beneficiaries of an estate can change the Will to make or increase a donation to a charity so the estate meets the 10% test.

Opt out of paying the reduced rate

If you're the executor of a Will or administrator of an estate, you can choose to pay IHT at 40% rather than the reduced rate – if the beneficiaries agree.

This can make it easier to deal with the estate, for example, if the cost of getting some of the assets professionally valued would outweigh the benefits of paying the reduced rate.

An estate doesn't have to pay IHT on any gifts given to charities, museums, universities or community amateur sports clubs

LIVING OUTSIDE THE UK

What happens when someone dies?

When someone living abroad dies, the rules for paying Inheritance Tax usually depend on:
* How long they lived abroad
* Whether their assets (property, money and possessions) are in the UK or abroad

If their assets in the UK are
* 'excluded assets'
* If their assets were put into a trust
* How long the deceased lived abroad

For IHT purposes, HM Revenue and Customs (HMRC) can treat someone who had their permanent home ('domicile') abroad as if it was in the UK (known as 'deemed domicile') if they had either:
* Had their permanent home in the UK at any time in the three years before they died
* Been resident in the UK for at least 17 of the 20 Income Tax years up to their death

If the deceased is deemed domiciled in the UK, their estate has to pay UK IHT on all their assets.

If they aren't deemed domiciled, their estate:
* Has to pay IHT on their assets (except excluded assets) in the UK
* Won't have to pay UK IHT on their assets outside the UK

HMRC only recognises a change of domicile if there's strong evidence that someone has permanently left the UK and intends to live abroad indefinitely.

UK assets you don't pay Inheritance Tax on

The estate doesn't have to pay IHT on some assets in the UK if the deceased was domiciled abroad. These are known as 'excluded assets'. They include:
- Holdings in authorised unit trusts and open-ended investment companies (OEICs)
- Foreign currency accounts with a bank or the Post Office
- UK government gilts which were issued 'free of tax to residents abroad'
- Overseas pensions
- Pay and possessions of members of visiting armed forces and staff of allied headquarters
- Government gilts

There's no IHT payable on government gilts issued:
- Before 30 April 1996 – and the deceased wasn't deemed domiciled or resident in the UK
- On or after 30 April 1996 – and the deceased wasn't resident in the UK, Channel Islands and Isle of Man

National Savings Certificates or certain other forms of small savings are excluded from IHT if the deceased was domiciled (not deemed domiciled) in the Channel Islands or the Isle of Man.

Double-taxation treaties

You may be able to avoid or reclaim tax through a double-taxation treaty if IHT is charged on the same assets by the UK and the country where the deceased lived.

Trusts

There are different rules if the deceased put assets outside the UK into a trust while they were domiciled in the UK.

A Will Is The First Step

Sharing out your estate

Planning your finances in advance should help you ensure that when you die, everything you own goes where you want it to. Making a Will is the first step in ensuring that your estate is shared out exactly as you want it to be.

If you don't make a Will, there are rules for sharing out your estate called the 'Law of Intestacy', which could mean your money going to family members who may not need it, with your unmarried partner or a partner with whom you are not in a registered civil partnership receiving nothing at all.

If you leave everything to your spouse or registered civil partner, there'll be no Inheritance Tax to pay because they are classed as an exempt beneficiary. Alternatively, you may decide to use your tax-free allowance to give some of your estate to someone else, or to a family trust.

Good reasons to make a Will

A Will sets out who is to benefit from your property and possessions (your estate) after your death. There are many good reasons to make a Will:
- You can decide how your assets are shared – if you don't have a Will, the law says who gets what
- If you're an unmarried couple (whether or not it's a same-sex relationship), you can make sure your partner is provided for
- If you're divorced, you can decide whether to leave anything to your former partner
- You can make sure you don't pay more Inheritance Tax than necessary

Before you write a Will it's a good idea to think about what you want included in it.

You should consider:
- How much money and what property and possessions you have
- Who do you want to benefit – your spouse or partner, children or other friends and relations? They become known as the beneficiaries who should look after any children under 18 years of age
- How much do you want to give them? You can either give a named legacy – such as a family heirloom or treasured item – or a monetary gift
- How do you own your home? If you own it as 'tenants in common' with your spouse or partner, then you each own a percentage that can be left to another person on death. Owning a property as 'joint tenants' means that you both own 100% and it solely belongs to the other on your death. Different property ownership rules apply in Scotland
- Who do you want to look after any of your children under the age of 18 when you die? They will become their legal guardians
- Who do you want to administer your Will when you die? They're called 'executors', and their tasks include collecting in any outstanding debts to your estate, paying off any loans and IHT due, and then paying out what is left according to your wishes. Many couples name their partner as executor, but it could be worth choosing a second one in case you should both die at the same time
- Do you want to put your money into trust when you die to provide an income and capital for your dependants? If you do, consider getting professional financial advice about the best trust to use
- Who will look after the trust? A trustee can either be a family member or friend, or a professional such as a solicitor

Passing on your estate

An executor is the person responsible for passing on your estate. You can appoint an executor by naming them in your Will. The courts can also appoint other people to be responsible for doing this job.

Once you've made your Will it is important to keep it in a safe place and tell your executor, close friend or relative where it is.

It is advisable to review your Will every five years and after any major change in your life, such as getting separated, married or divorced, having a child, or moving house. Any change must be by codicil (an addition, amendment or supplement to a Will) or by making a new Will.

Scottish law on inheritance differs from English law.

If you don't make a Will, there are rules for sharing out your estate called the 'Law of Intestacy', which could mean your money going to family members who may not need it, with your unmarried partner or a partner with whom you are not in a registered civil partnership receiving nothing at all.

Chapter 12

It's A Changing Financial World - Five Tips On What To Do With Your Money

Yields are low. Markets are volatile. Confidence is scarce.

It's fair to say that the investment world looks daunting - opportunities seem thin on the ground and some long-relied upon investment approaches may no longer work - but the good news is there are still some opportunities out there.

To make these opportunities work, we believe your portfolio must be flexible enough to adapt to rapidly changing markets and more diverse than it's ever been before.

This may mean investing in a broader array of investments and diversifying both across geographies and asset classes and within them, creating a more dynamic, diverse portfolio.

Read on to find out five tips on what to do with your money.

1. Rethink the Cost of Cash

While holding cash protects capital, in the long run low interest rates leave the value of money susceptible to inflation, reducing purchasing power in years to come.

In today's uncertain markets many investors have switched into what they view as a riskless trade - cash. So much so, banks and building societies can be considered safe and cash deposits protect your capital and offer more predictable returns.

Even with low inflation returns on cash have not always kept up with the cost of living. While holding some cash is wise, it may not be the right way to save in the long run given our low interest rate environment and the erosive effects of inflation.

Assuming a 3% inflation rate, £100,000 in cash would be worth the equivalent of £47,761 in 25 years' time in terms of purchasing power if we ignore the effects of interest income.

What to do with your money?

A traditional safe haven, cash protects your capital, but over the long run it may not meet your goals especially when interest rates are below inflation.

Whilst today's market conditions understandably produce anxiety, investors with large amounts of cash should take a step back, reassess their goals and risk tolerance, and work with their financial advisers to make their money work harder.

Erosion of Purchasing Power

Impact of Hypothetical 3% Annual Inflation Rate (assuming no interest return for simplicity) on the Real Value of Cash.

2. Go Further for Income

If traditional fixed income products fail to keep up with inflation, investors may consider taking on more risk and choosing assets such as company dividends and corporate bonds.

The hunt for reliable investment income has rarely been more challenging. In many countries low interest rates means leaving money in the bank offers negligible returns.

Meanwhile, yields on traditional fixed income investments such as US treasuries, UK gilts and German bonds are at all-time lows. Investors are left to wonder where to find income streams that stay ahead of inflation while remaining comfortable with the risk they take on.

While inflation erodes the purchasing power of cash and most traditional bonds, equity dividend growth has historically kept pace with inflation.

What to do with your money?

The good news is that there are sustainable and even rising income streams out there, for those who know where to look and have the risk appetite to act. It may mean embracing a different asset class or even considering new opportunities in familiar places.

The Case for Dividends

Company shares which pay dividends, are an attractive income option.

At the moment, the yield (through dividend payments) on many shares is more than twice that on traditional government bonds. Furthermore, unlike the fixed payments on many bonds dividends can increase over time – and in fact have historically done so at a rate that keeps up with inflation, providing real (inflation adjusted) income.

Alongside this, scope for the share price to rise offers potential for long-term capital growth. Of course, there are no guarantees that equity income investment will provide an effective hedge against inflation in the future and your capital and income is at risk.

Look to Corporate Debt

For investors prepared to take on more risk, many corporate bonds offer attractive income opportunities today. Of course, corporate bonds offer higher yields than US Treasuries as they have a higher chance of default (not paying back the money they owe).

However, for those who do their homework and identify strong balance sheets and robust business models, there are compelling investment stories behind some of these bonds.

Company balance sheets have rarely been stronger than they are today and with bank lending hampered, companies are increasingly turning to bond markets to raise capital.

Global High Dividend Yield and High Dividend Growth Shares Have Outperformed the Rest of the Stock Market

Annualised average % total returns from 1988 to 2011 of shares in the MSCI AC World Index in sterling terms.

Past performance is not a guide to future performance and should not be the sole factor of consideration when selecting an investment.

3. Open Your Eyes to Alternatives

Many asset classes and investing techniques historically considered the preserve of institutional investors are now more widely available. These carry their own risks but tend to generate different returns to traditional investments, helping diversify portfolios.

The age-old adage "don't put all your eggs in one basket" is often a good rule of thumb when constructing your investment portfolio. Investing in the broadest set of opportunities as possible – across markets, asset classes and styles – often helps to smooth returns, thereby reducing risk.

We believe that creating a dynamic portfolio, one that is more diverse than ever before, is an essential step to helping investors mitigate against potential future losses. An allocation o these additional diversifiers, such as alternative investments, is one way to achieve this goal.

The size of the Absolute Return UCITS Fund industry in Europe has almost quadrupled in under three years, growing from $22bn of assets under management in January 2009 to $84bn in September 2011.*

*Source: Morgan Stanley as at 30 September 2011

What to do with your money?

Investments that offer superior diversification – such as property, commodities or absolute return strategies – are no longer the preserve of the most sophisticated investors.

Carefully blending a variety of these investments to a traditional portfolio has the potential to enhance returns while also reducing risk because they don't typically move in chorus with the other components of a portfolio. These are also more accessible than ever through unit trusts and exchange traded funds (ETFs).

4. Be Active About Passive

Exchange traded funds (ETFs) and traditional index tracker funds provide a transparent and low-cost way to tap into market returns and gain access to asset classes and global markets.

Financial experts have long debated whether investors should be either active or passive. The answer is not active or passive: it's both.

Investors can combine both types of investments to create diversified portfolios. Passive investing is a low cost and efficient way to gain exposure to global markets and sectors. Active investing has scope to outperform the returns of a market through fund manager's skill. Both have their own merits and your financial adviser can help you decide the right balance between them for your portfolio.

Increasingly investors are blending active and passive funds, combining the merits of both approaches while helping to manage risk and cost.

What to do with your money?

Passive investments can take the form of traditional index tracking funds and exchange traded funds (ETFs).

Index tracking funds aim to mirror the performance of an index, such as the FTSE 100 Index of leading UK blue-chip shares. They offer investors low cost, efficient market exposure. Like traditional funds, they price on a daily basis. ETFs are also managed to accurately mirror the performance of an index, such as the FTSE 100 Index of leading UK blue-chip shares.

They are collective investments but can be bought and sold on a stock exchange like a share in a company, allowing investors to adjust their portfolios nimbly and efficiently as markets shift.

ETFs are often used as a flexible cost-efficient way to invest and increase access to markets that can be difficult or expensive to enter such as alternatives and emerging markets.

Core/satellite investing

Core/satellite investing is based on the simple concept of splitting a portfolio into two segments. Passive funds are sometimes used as a core part of an investor's portfolio and sometimes as satellites.

Satellite investments are typically used for exposure to more specialised asset classes and markets. Investors can work with their financial advisers to determine the appropriate balance for their portfolio.

5. Use Your Longevity

We are living longer. This allows investors to expand their investment horizon well beyond the day they retire and perhaps keep some carefully tailored exposure to risk assets such as equities for longer than they may have in the past.

As life spans increase, many investors worry they will outlive their savings. With longer retirements than ever before they may need to rethink their pension ideas. Retirement used to be a single life-stage. However, it makes more sense now to think about retirement as having several phases, each with slightly different financial needs. Investors can now expand their investment time horizons well beyond the date they retire and generate long-term returns to retain the lifestyle they want.

A healthy couple aged 65 in the United States now has a 50% chance that at least one of them will live to the age of 92, and a 25% chance that one of them will reach 97.

Source: Annuity 2000 Mortality table, Society of Actuaries, US. Figures assume you are in good health.

What to do with your money?

Living well in older age is about building smart, dynamic, diverse and global portfolios. It is about investing across more asset classes for specific needs or "outcomes", "fulfilling a long held dream" or simply achieving the kind of retirement you want.

Investors should consider maintaining some carefully tailored exposure to risk assets, such as company shares, for longer than retirees have done in the past. Investors of all ages should consider ways to keep their money working harder to help them achieve their goals.

For more information, contact Hartey Wealth Management on 0808 168 5866, or email info@harteywm.co.uk

The contents of this book provide information on the matters you may want to consider when reviewing your financial affairs and do not constitute advice. Hartey Wealth Management is authorised and regulated by the Financial Conduct Authority and can provide formal advice if required.

There are references to Tax rates, reliefs and regulations in the book. These were those applicable at the time of publication (December 2015) and are subject to change.

Registered in England and Wales No:8288660. Registered Office: Hilliards Court, Chester Business Park, Chester CH4 9QP. Hartey Wealth Management Ltd are authorised and regulated by the Financial Conduct Authority.

Chapter 13
Glossary of Financial Terms

A

Alpha

Alpha is a measure of a fund's over or under performance compared to its benchmark. It represents the return of the fund when the benchmark is assumed to have a return of zero. It shows the extra value that the manager's activities seem to have contributed. If the Alpha is 5, the fund has outperformed its benchmark by 5% and the greater the Alpha, the greater the out performance.

Alternative Assets

Includes private real estate, public real estate, venture capital, non-venture private equity, hedge funds, distressed securities, oil and gas partnerships, event arbitrage, general arbitrage, managed funds, commodities, timber and other.

American Stock Exchange

AMEX is the second-largest stock exchange in the U.S., after the New York Stock Exchange (NYSE). In general, the listing rules are a little more lenient than those of the NYSE, and thus the AMEX has a larger representation of stocks and bonds issued by smaller companies than the NYSE. Some index options and interest rate options trading also occurs on the AMEX. The AMEX started as an alternative to the NYSE. It originated when brokers began meeting on the curb outside the NYSE in order to trade stocks that failed to meet the Big Board's stringent listing requirements, but the AMEX now has its own trading floor. In 1998, the parent company of the NASDAQ purchased the AMEX and combined their markets, although the two continue to operate separately. Also called The Curb.

Annual Rate of Return

There are several ways of calculating this. The most commonly used methodologies reflect the compounding effect of each period's increase or decrease from the previous period.

Annual Percentage Rate (APR)

The APR is designed to measure the "true cost of a loan". The aim is to create a level playing field for lenders preventing them from advertising a low rate and hiding fees. In the case of a mortgage the APR should reflect the yearly cost of a mortgage, including interest, mortgage insurance, and the origination fee, expressed as a percentage.

Annual Premium Equivalent

Calculated as regular premiums plus 10% of single premiums.

Arbitrage

A financial transaction or strategy that seeks to profit from a price differential perceived with respect to related or correlated instruments in different markets. Typically involves the simultaneous purchase of an instrument in one market and the sale of the same or related instrument in another market.

Asset Allocation

Apportioning of investment funds among categories of assets such as cash equivalents, stock, fixed-income investments, alternative investments such as hedge funds and managed futures funds, and tangible assets like real estate, precious metals and collectibles.

Average Monthly Gain

The average of all the profitable months of the fund.

Average Monthly Loss

The average of all the negative months of the fund.

Average Monthly Return

The average of all the monthly performance numbers of the fund.

B

Basis Point
A basis point is one one-hundredth of a percent i.e. 50 basis points or "bps" is 0.5%.

Bear / Bear Market
Bear is a term describing an investor who thinks that a market will decline. The term also refers to a short position held by a market maker. A Bear Market is a market where prices are falling over an extended period.

Bellwether
A stock or bond that is widely believed to be an indicator of the overall market's condition. Also known as Barometer stock.

Beta
Beta is a measure of a fund's volatility compared to its benchmark, or how sensitive it is to market movements. A fund with a Beta close to 1 means that the fund will move generally in line with the benchmark. Higher than 1 and the fund is more volatile than the benchmark, so that with a Beta of 1.5, say, the fund will be expected to rise or fall 1.5 points for every 1 point of benchmark movement. If this Beta is an advantage in a rising market – a 15% gain for every 10% rise in the benchmark –the reverse is true when markets fall. This is when managers will look for Betas below 1, so that in a down market the fund will not perform as badly as its benchmark.

Bid Price
The price at which an investor may sell units of a fund back to the fund manager. It is also the price at which a market maker will buy shares.

Blue Chips
Large, continuously well performing stock, presumed to be among the safer investments on an exchange.

Bond

A debt investment, with which the investor loans money to an entity (company or Government) that borrows the funds for a defined period of time at a specified interest rate. The indebted entity issues investors a certificate, or bond, that states the interest rate (coupon rate) that will be paid and when the loaned funds are to be returned (maturity date). Interest on bonds is usually paid every six-months.

Bond Rating Codes

Rating	S&P	Moody's
Highest quality	AAA	Aaa
High quality	AA	Aa
Upper medium quality	A	A
Medium grade	BBB	Baa
Somewhat speculative	BB	Ba
Low grade, speculative	B	B
Low grade, default possible	CCC	Caa
Low grade, partial recovery possible	CC	Ca
Default, recovery unlikely	C	C

Bottom up Investing

An approach to investing which seeks to identify well performing individual securities before considering the impact of economic trends.

BRIC

A term used to refer to the combination of Brazil, Russia, India and China. General consensus is that the term was first prominently used in a thesis of the Goldman Sachs Investment Bank. The main point of this 2003 paper was to argue that the economies of the BRICs are rapidly developing and by the year 2050 will eclipse most of the current richest countries of the world. Due to the popularity of the Goldman

Sachs thesis, "BRIC" and "BRIMC" (M for Mexico), these terms are also extended to "BRICS" (S for South Africa) and "BRICKET" (including Eastern Europe and Turkey) and have become more generic terms to refer to these emerging markets.

Bull / Bull Market

An investor who believes that the market is likely to rise. A Bull Market is a market where prices are rising over an extended period.

Bulldog Bond

A sterling denominated bond that is issued in London by a company that is not British. These sterling bonds are referred to as bulldog bonds as the bulldog is a national symbol of England.

C

Child Trust Fund

A Child Trust Fund is a savings and investment account for children. Children born on or after 1st September 2002 will receive a £250 voucher to start their account. The account belongs to the child and can't be touched until they turn 18, so that children have some money behind them to start their adult life. Payments or contributions can be made up to a maximum of £1,200 per 12 month period (starting on the birthday of the child), excluding the voucher amount. Interest and capital growth will be earned tax-free. Additional deposits can be made by parents, grandparents or anyone else.

Closed-end Fund

Type of fund that has a fixed number of shares or units. Unlike open-ended mutual funds, closed-end funds do not stand ready to issue and redeem shares on a continuous basis.

Collar

A contract that protects the holder from a rise or fall in interest rates or some other underlying security above or below certain fixed points. The contract offers the investor protection from interest rate moves outside of an expected range.

Constant Proportion Portfolio Insurance CPPI

Strategy that basically buys shares as they rise and sells shares as they fall. To implement a CPPI strategy, the investor selects a floor below which the portfolio value is not allowed to fall. The floor increases in value at the rate of return on cash. If you think of the difference between the assets and floor as a "cushion", then the CPPI decision rule is to simply keep the exposure to shares a constant multiple of the cushion.

Consumer Discretionary Sector

The array of businesses included in the Consumer Discretionary Sector are categorized into five industry groups. They are: Automobiles and Components; Consumer Durables and Apparel; Hotels, Restaurants and Leisure; Media; and Retailing.

Consumer Staples

The industries that manufacture and sell food/beverages, tobacco, prescription drugs and household products. Proctor and Gamble would be considered a consumer staple company because many of its products are household and food related.

Convertible Arbitrage

This is an investment strategy that involves taking a long position on a convertible security and a short position in its converting common stock. This strategy attempts to exploit profits when there is a pricing error made in the conversion factor of the convertible security.

Convertible Bond

A bond that can be exchanged, at the option of the holder, for a specific number of shares of the company's preferred stock or common stock. Convertibility affects the performance of the bond in certain ways. First and foremost, convertible bonds tend to have lower interest rates than nonconvertibles because they also accrue value as the price of the underlying stock rises. In this way, convertible bonds offer some of the benefits of both stocks and bonds. Convertibles earn interest even when the stock is trading down or sideways, but when the stock prices rise, the value of the convertible increases. Therefore, convertibles can offer protection against a decline in stock price. Because they are sold at a premium over the price of the stock, convertibles should be expected to earn that premium back in the first three or four years after purchase.

Core Fund

Fund that takes a middle of the road approach to generate returns for shareholders. These funds are generally structured in two ways. One strategy is to combine stocks and bonds (and possible income trusts) into a single fund to achieve a steady return and improved asset allocation. The other approach is to combine growth stocks and value stocks to diversify the risk from the typical ups and downs of markets. This type of fund can also be called a blend fund since it can show characteristics of a pure growth fund or a pure value fund. Either way, a core fund is focused to producing long-term results.

Corporate Bonds

Corporate Bonds are similar to gilts but are a form of borrowing by companies rather than Governments. Let's say Astra Zeneca wished to borrow a billion pounds for research and development. They would initially approach their brokers who would review the strength of Astra Zeneca versus the Government to assess what is a reasonable "risk premium". A secure company might be able to borrow money at 1 or 2 percentage points above the gilt rate and a very insecure company may have to pay 10 percentage points above the Government rate or in some cases substantially more. Companies' security is generally graded from AAA to no rating, the less secure debt being known in the UK as "High Yield", or as it is more accurately described by Americans as "Junk Bonds". So with Corporate Bonds the short term returns will vary in line with interest rates as they do with gilts, but also in line with the perceived strength of the company.

Correlation

A standardised measure of the relative movement between two variables, such as the price of a fund and an index. The degree of correlation between two variables is measured on a scale of −1 to +1. If two variables move up or down together, they are positively correlated. If they tend to move in opposite directions, they are negatively correlated.

Coupon

Denotes the rate of interest on a fixed interest security. A 10 % coupon pays interest of 10 % a year on the nominal value of the stock.

Cyclical Stock

The stock of a company which is sensitive to business cycles and whose performance is strongly tied to the overall economy. Cyclical companies tend to make products or provide services that are in lower demand during downturns in the economy and higher demand during upswings. Examples include the automobile, steel, and housing industries. The stock price of a cyclical company will often rise just before an economic upturn begins, and fall just before a downturn begins. Investors in cyclical stocks try to make the largest gains by buying the stock at the bottom of a business cycle, just before a turnaround begins. Opposite of defensive stock.

D

Debenture

A loan raised by a company, paying a fixed rate of interest and secured on the assets of the company.

Defensive Stock

A stock that tends to remain stable under difficult economic conditions. Defensive stocks include food, tobacco, oil, and utilities. These stocks hold up in hard times because demand does not decrease as dramatically as it may in other sectors. Defensive stocks tend to lag behind the rest of the market during economic expansion because demand does not increase as dramatically in an upswing.

Delta

The rate at which the price of an option changes in response to a move in the price of the underlying security. If an option's delta is 0.5 (out of a maximum of 1), a $2 move in the price of the underlying will produce a $1 move in the option.

Delta Hedge

A hedging position that causes a portfolio to be delta neutral.

Derivatives

Financial contracts whose value is tied to an underlying asset. Derivatives include futures and options.

Discount

When a security is selling below its normal market price, opposite of premium.

Distressed Securities

A distressed security is a security of a company which is currently in default, bankruptcy, financial distress or a turnaround situation.

E

Efficient Frontier

A line created from the risk-reward graph, comprised of optimal portfolios. The optimal portfolios plotted along the curve have the highest expected return possible for the given amount of risk.

EFTA – European Fair Trade Association

A network of 11 Fair Trade organisations in nine European countries which import Fair Trade products from some 400 economically disadvantaged producer groups in Africa, Asia and Latin America. EFTA's members are based in Austria,

Belgium, France, Germany, Italy, the Netherlands, Spain, Switzerland and the United Kingdom.

Embedded Value EV
A method of accounting used by life insurance business. The embedded value is the sum of the net assets of the insurance business under conventional accounting and the present value of the in-force business based on estimates of future cash flows and conservative assumptions about for example, mortality, persistence and expenses. Accounts users prefer this method because it gives a separate indication of new business profitability, a key performance indicator for a life insurer.

Emerging Markets
Typically includes markets within countries that have an underdeveloped or developing infrastructure with significant potential for economic growth and increased capital market participation for foreign investors. These countries generally possess some of the following characteristics; per capita GNP less than $9000, recent economic liberalisation, debt ratings below investment grade, recent liberalisation of the political system and non membership of the Organisation of Economic Cooperation and Development. Because many emerging countries do not allow short selling or offer viable futures or other derivatives products with which to hedge, emerging market investing entails investing in geographic regions that have underdeveloped capital markets and exhibit high growth rates and high rates of inflation. Investing in emerging markets can be very volatile and may also involve currency risk, political risk and liquidity risk. Generally a long-only investment strategy.

Emerging Markets Debt
Debt instruments of emerging market countries. Most bonds are US Dollar denominated and a majority of secondary market trading is in Brady bonds.

Equities
Ownership positions in companies that can be traded in public markets. Often produce current income which is paid in

the form of quarterly dividends. In the event of the company going bankrupt equity holders' claims are subordinate to the claims of preferred stockholders and bondholders.

Equity Hedge
Also known as long / short equity, combines core long holdings of equities with short sales of stock or stock index options. Equity hedge portfolios may be anywhere from net long to net short depending on market conditions. Equity hedge managers generally increase net long exposure in bull markets and decrease net long exposure or are even net short in a bear market.

Equity Market Neutral
This investment strategy is designed to exploit equity market inefficiencies and usually involves being simultaneously long and short equity portfolios of the same size within a country. Market neutral portfolios are designed to be either beta or currency neutral or both. Attempts are often made to control industry, sector and market capitalisation exposures.

Equity Risk
The risk of owning stock or having some other form of ownership interest.

Ethical Investing
Choosing to invest in companies that operate ethically, provide social benefits, and are sensitive to the environment. Also called socially conscious investing.

EU
European Union. The economic association of over a dozen European countries which seek to create a unified, barrier-free market for products and services throughout the continent. The majority of countries share a common currency with a unified authority over that currency. Notable exceptions to the common currency are the UK, Sweden, Norway, Denmark.

Eurobond

A bond issued and traded outside the country whose currency it is denominated in, and outside the regulations of a single country; usually a bond issued by a non-European company for sale in Europe. Interest is paid gross.

Eurozone or Euroland

The collective group of countries which use the Euro as their common currency.

Event Driven Investing

Investment strategy seeking to identify and exploit pricing inefficiencies that have been caused by some sort of corporate event such as a merger, spin-off, distressed situation or recapitalisation.

Exit Fee

A fee paid to redeem an investment. It is a charge levied for cashing in a fund's capital.

Exposure

The condition of being subjected to a source of risk.

F

FCP

Fonds Commun de Placement. FCPs are a common fund structure in Luxembourg. In contrast to SICAV, they are not companies, but are organised as co-ownerships and must be managed by a fund management company.

Feeder Fund

A fund which invests only in another fund. The feeder fund may be a different currency to the main fund and may be used to channel cash in to the main fund for a different currency class.

Fixed Interest

The term fixed interest is often used by banks and building societies relating to an account that pays a set rate of interest for a set time period. This type of investment is capital secure and the returns are known at outset. However, fixed interest within the investment world is a completely different concept. It is used to describe funds that invest in Government Gilts and Corporate Bond securities.

Fixed Income Arbitrage

Investment strategy that seeks to exploit pricing inefficiencies in fixed income securities and their derivative instruments. Typical investment is long a fixed income security or related instrument that is perceived to be undervalued and short a similar related fixed income security or related instrument. Often highly leveraged.

Floating Rate

Any interest rate that changes on a periodic basis. The change is usually tied to movement of an outside indicator, such as the Bank of England Base Rate. Movement above or below certain levels is often prevented by a predetermined floor and ceiling for a given rate. For example, you might see a rate set at "base plus 2%". This means that the rate on the loan will always be 2% higher than the base rate, which changes regularly to take into account changes in the inflation rate. For an individual taking out a loan when rates are low, a fixed rate loan would allow him or her to "lock in" the low rates and not be concerned with fluctuations. On the other hand, if interest rates were historically high at the time of the loan, he or she would benefit from a floating rate loan, because as the prime rate fell to historically normal levels, the rate on the loan would decrease. Also called adjustable rate.

Floor

A contract that protects the holder against a decline in interest rates or prices below a certain point.

Forward

An agreement to execute a transaction at some time in the future. In the foreign exchange market this is a tailor made deal where an investor agrees to buy or sell an amount of currency at a given date.

Forward Rate Agreement (FRA)
A type of forward contract that is linked to interest rates.

FTSE 100
The Financial Times Stock Exchange 100 stock index, a market cap weighted index of stocks traded on the London Stock Exchange. Similar to the S&P 500 in the United States.

Fund of Funds
An investment vehicle that invests in more than one fund. Portfolio will typically diversify across a variety of investment managers, investment strategies and subcategories. Provides investors with access to managers with higher minimums than individuals might otherwise afford.

Funds under Management
Total amount of funds managed by an entity, excluding

G

Gearing
The effect that borrowing has on the equity capital of a company or the asset value of a fund. If the assets bought with funds borrowed appreciate in value, the excess of value over funds borrowed will accrue to the shareholder, thus augmenting, or gearing up the value of their investment.

Geographic Spread
The distribution in a fund's portfolio over different parts of the world, either by countries or larger areas.

Gilt-Edged Securities
Stocks and shares issued and guaranteed by the British government to raise funds and traded on the Stock Exchange. A relatively risk-free investment, gilts bear fixed interest and are usually redeemable on a specified date. The term is now used generally to describe securities of the highest value. According to the redemption date, gilts are described as short (up to five

years),   medium,   or   long   (15 years or more).

Gilts

Gilts are effectively Government borrowing. When the Chancellor does not have sufficient income to meet his expenditure, then the Government will often borrow money in the form of gilts. These can be for a variety of different terms, paying a range of interest rates.

A typical example would be a ten year gilt which may pay, say, 5% income. This is the most secure investment you could buy, as you know the rate of return and you know when you will receive your capital back. The UK Government has never defaulted on a gilt.

If however you wanted to access your money before maturity then you would have to sell your gilt on the open market. Let's say you were trying to sell your gilt after one year. In order to obtain a value any potential purchaser will look at the term remaining on your gilt and the interest rate promised, and compare this to new gilts being launched at the time. If the Government was then launching a new gilt over a nine year time period, and promising to pay 6% per annum, then clearly nobody is going to want to pay the same amount of money for your gilt which is offering a lower interest rate.

They would probably therefore offer at least 9% less than you originally paid for it to reflect the 1% difference in income over the nine years of the remaining term. So whilst you had set out to achieve guaranteed returns, if you sell a gilt before maturity you could potentially make a capital loss on it, in this instance a loss of 9% over the year.

However, if you decide to keep the gilt until its maturity you will still receive all of your interest and the capital back. Having said this, your valuation each year will vary depending on market conditions.

GNMA (Ginnie Mae)

Government National Mortgage Association. A U.S. Government-owned agency which buys mortgages from lending institutions, securitizes them, and then sells them to investors. Because the payments to investors are guaranteed by the full faith and credit of the U.S. Government, they return slightly less interest than other mortgage-backed securities.

Growth Stocks
Stock of a company which is growing earnings and/or revenue faster than its industry or the overall market. Such companies usually pay little or no dividends, preferring to use the income instead to finance further expansion.

Growth Orientated Portfolios
Dominant theme is growth in revenues, earnings and market share. Many of these portfolios are hedged to mitigate against declines in the overall market.

Global Macro
The investment strategy is based on shifts in global economies. Derivatives are often used to speculate on currency and interest rate movements.

Guided Architecture
In relation to funds, for example FPIL Premier policyholders may only go into the FPIL mirror fund range – this is guided architecture. In contrast to FPIL Reserve policyholders who may choose any security – open architecture.

H

Hawk
An investor who has a negative view towards inflation and its effects on markets. Hawkish investors prefer higher interest rates in order to maintain reduced inflation.

Hedge

Any transaction with the objective of limiting exposure to risk such as changes in exchange rates or prices.

Hedge Fund

A pooled investment vehicle that is privately organised, administered by investment management professionals and generally not widely available to the general public. Many hedge funds share a number of characteristics; they hold long and short positions, use leverage to enhance returns, pay performance or incentive fees to their managers, have high minimum investment requirements and target absolute returns. Generally, hedge funds are not constrained by legal limitations on their investment discretion and can adopt a variety of trading strategies. The hedge fund manager often has its own capital (or that of its principals) invested in the hedge fund it manages.

Herding

Hedge fund managers while taking a position may encourage other investors to follow this trend.

High Conviction Stock Picking

A typical portfolio is not constrained by benchmarks, allowing the manager to pursue an approach where a smaller number of stocks are chosen that may bear little or no resemblance to the consensus view. i.e the manager's conviction.

High Water Mark

The assurance that a fund only takes fees on profits actually earned by an individual investment. For example, a £10 million investment is made in year one and the fund declines by 50%, leaving £5 million in the fund. In year two, the fund returns 100% bringing the investment value back to £10 million. If a fund has a high water mark it will not take incentive fees on the return in year two since the investment has never grown. The fund will only take incentive fees if the investment grows above the initial level of £10 million.

High-Yield Bond
Often called junk bonds, these are low grade fixed income securities of companies that show significant upside potential. The bond has to pay a high yield due to significant credit risk.

Hurdle Rate
The minimum investment return a fund must exceed before a performance-based incentive fee can be taken. For example if a fund has a hurdle rate of 10% and the fund returned 18% for the year, the fund will only take incentive fees on the 8 percentage points above the hurdle rate.

I

Index
An arithmetic mean of selected stocks intended to represent the behaviour of the market or some component of it. One example is the FTSE 100 which adds the current prices of the one hundred FTSE 100 stocks and divides the results by a pre-determined number, the divisor.

Index Funds
A fund that attempts to achieve a performance similar to that stated in an index. The purpose of this fund is to realise an investment return at least equal to the broad market covered by the indices while reducing management costs.

Index Linked Gilt
A gilt, the interest and capital of which change in line with the Retail Price Index.

In the Money
A condition where an option has a positive intrinsic value.

Intrinsic Value
A component of the market value of an option. If the strike price of a call option is cheaper than the prevailing market price, then the option has a positive intrinsic value, and is "in the money".

Investment Grade

Something classified as investment grade is, by implication, medium to high quality.

1) In the case of a stock, a firm that has a strong balance sheet, considerable capitalization, and is recognized as a leader in its industry.

2) In the case of fixed income, a bond with a rating of BBB or higher.

J

January Effect

Tendency of US stock markets to rise between December 31 and the end of the first week in January. The January Effect occurs because many investors choose to sell some of their stock right before the end of the year in order to claim a capital loss for tax purposes. Once the tax calendar rolls over to a new year on January 1st these same investors quickly reinvest their money in the market, causing stock prices to rise. Although the January Effect has been observed numerous times throughout history, it is difficult for investors to profit from it since the market as a whole expects it to happen and therefore adjusts its prices accordingly.

Junk Bond

A bond that pays a high yield due to significant credit risk

L

Leverage

When investors borrow funds to increase the amount they have invested in a particular position, they use leverage. Sometimes managers use leverage to enable them to put on new positions without having to take off other positions prematurely. Managers who target very small price discrepancies or spreads will often use leverage to magnify the returns from these discrepancies. Leverage both magnifies the risk of the strategy as well as creates risk by giving the lender power over the disposition of the investment portfolio. This may occur in the form of increased margin requirements or adverse market shifts, forcing a partial or complete liquidation of the portfolio.

The amount of leverage used by the fund is commonly expressed as a percentage of the fund. For example if the fund has £1 million and borrows another £2 million to bring the total invested to £3 million, then the fund is leveraged 200%

Life Cycle Funds

Life-cycle funds are the closest thing the industry has to a maintenance-free retirement fund. Life-cycle funds, also referred to as "age-based funds" or "target-date funds", are a special breed of the balanced fund. They are a type of fund of funds structured between equity and fixed income. But the distinguishing feature of the life-cycle fund is that its overall asset allocation automatically adjusts to become more conservative as your expected retirement date approaches. While life-cycle funds have been around for a while, they have been gaining popularity.

LIBOR

London Inter Bank Offered Rate.

Liquidity

1) The degree to which an asset or security can be bought or sold in the market without affecting the asset's price. Liquidity is characterized by a high level of trading activity.

2) The ability to convert an asset to cash quickly.

Investing in illiquid assets is riskier because there might not be a way for you to get your money out of the investment. Examples of assets with good liquidity include blue chip common stock and those assets in the money market. A fund with good liquidity would be characterised by having enough units outstanding to allow large
transactions without a substantial change in price.

Liquidity Risk

Risk from a lack of liquidity, ie an investor having difficulty getting their money out of an investment.

Listed Security
Stock or bond that has been accepted for trading by an organised and registered securities exchange. Advantages of being listed are an orderly market place, more liquidity, fair price determination, accurate and continuous reporting on sales and quotations, information on listed companies and strict regulations for the protection of securities holders.

Lock Up / Lock In
Time period during which an initial investment cannot be redeemed.

Long Position
Holding a positive amount of an asset (or an asset underlying a derivative instrument)

Long / Short Hedged
Also described as the Jones Model. Manager buys securities he believes will go up in price and sells short securities he believes will decline in price. Manager will be either net long or net short and may change the net position frequently. For example a manager may be 60% long and 100% short, giving him a market exposure of 40% net short. The basic belief behind this strategy is that it will enhance the manager's stock picking ability and protect investors in all market conditions.

M

Macro-Economics
The field of economics that studies the behaviour of the economy as a whole. Macroeconomics looks at economy-wide phenomena such as changes in unemployment, national income, rate of growth, and price levels.

Managed Accounts

Accounts of individual investors which are managed individually by an investment manager. The minimum size is usually in excess of £3 million.

Managed Futures

An approach to fund management that uses positions in government securities, futures contracts, options on futures contracts and foreign exchange in a portfolio. Some managers specialise in physical commodity futures but most find they must trade a variety of financial and non-financial contracts if they have considerable assets under management.

Management Fee

The fees taken by the manager on the entire asset level of the investment. For example, if at the end of the period the investment is valued at £1 million and the management fee is 1.2%, then the fee would be £12,000.

Margin

The amount of assets that must be deposited in a margin account in order to secure a portion of a party's obligations under a contract. For example, to buy or sell an exchange traded futures contract, a party must post a specified amount that is determined by the exchange, referred to as initial margin. In addition, a party will be required to post variation margin if the futures contracts change in value. Margin is also required in connection with the purchase and sale of securities where the full purchase price is not paid up front or the securities sold are not owned by the seller.

Market Maker

An Exchange member firm that is obliged to make a continuous two way price, that is to offer to buy and sell securities in which it is registered throughout the mandatory quote period.

Market Neutral Investing

An investment strategy that aims to produce almost the same profit regardless of market circumstances, often by taking a combination of long and short positions. This approach relies on the manager's ability to make money through relative valuation analysis, rather than through market direction forecasting. The strategy attempts to eliminate market risk and be profitable in any market condition.

Market Risk
Risk from changes in market prices

Market Timing
1) An accepted practice of allocating assets among investments by switching into investments that appear to be beginning an up trend, and switching out of investments that appear to be starting a downtrend.

2) An increasingly unacceptable / illegal practice of undertaking frequent or large transactions in mutual funds. Especially where there is a time difference between the close of the relevant markets that the fund invests in and the valuation of the fund. ie a Far East fund that is valued the next day in the UK.

Market Value
The value at which an asset trades, or would trade in the market.

Mark to Market
When the value of securities in a portfolio are updated to reflect the changes that have occurred due to the movement of the underlying market. The security will then be valued at its current market price.

Maximum Draw Down
The largest loss suffered by a security or fund, peak to trough, over a given period, usually one month.

Merger Arbitrage
Sometimes called Risk Arbitrage, involves investment in event-driven situations such as leveraged buy outs, mergers and hostile takeovers. Normally the stock of an acquisition

target appreciates while the acquiring company's stock decreases in value.

Mezzanine Level
Stage of a company's development just prior to its going public. Venture capitalists entering at that point have a lower risk of loss than at previous stages and can look forward to early capital appreciation as a result of the market value gained by an initial public offering.

Micro-Economics
The behaviour and purchasing decisions of individuals and firms.

Money Market Funds
Mutual funds that invest in short term highly liquid money market instruments. These funds are used when preservation of capital is paramount. They may be used to "park" money between investments, especially during periods of market uncertainty.

Mortgage Backed Security
A pass-through security that aggregates a pool of mortgage-backed debt obligations. Mortgage-backed securities' principal amounts are usually government guaranteed. Homeowners' principal and interest payments pass from the originating bank through a government agency or investment bank, to investors, net of a loan servicing fee payable to the originator.

Multi-Manager Product
An investment pool that allocates assets to a number of managers with different investment styles. This methodology facilitates a high degree of diversification and accordingly the potential for a greater spread of risk. Hedge funds often have this structure. Smaller investors are able to enjoy access to a greater variety of managers that would normally be prohibited by minimum investment requirements for each manager. Funds of funds are a classic multi-manager product.

Municipal Bond (USA)

A debt security issued by a state, municipality, or county, in order to finance its capital expenditures. Municipal bonds are exempt from federal taxes and from most state and local taxes, especially if you live in the state the bond is issued. Such expenditures might include the construction of highways, bridges or schools. "Munis" are bought for their favourable tax implications, and are popular with people in high income tax brackets.

Mutual Fund

A security that gives small investors access to a well diversified portfolio of equities, bonds, and other securities. Each shareholder participates in the gain or loss of the fund. Shares are issued and can be redeemed as needed. The fund's net asset value (NAV) is determined each day. Each mutual fund portfolio is invested to match the objective stated in the prospectus. Some examples of mutual funds are UK Unit Trusts, Open-ended Investment Companies (OEICs), EU registered UCITS, Luzembourg based SICAVs.

N

NAREIT

National Association of Real Estate Investment Trusts

Nasdaq

A computerised system established by the NASD to facilitate trading by providing broker/dealers with current bid and ask price quotes on over-the-counter stocks and some listed stocks. Unlike the Amex and the NYSE, the Nasdaq (once an acronym for the National Association of securities Dealers Automated Quotation system) does not have a physical trading floor that brings together buyers and sellers. Instead, all trading on the Nasdaq exchange is done over a network of computers and telephones. Also, the Nasdaq does not employ market specialists to buy unfilled orders like the NYSE does. The Nasdaq began when brokers started informally trading via telephone; the network was later formalized and linked by computer in the early 1970s. In 1998 the parent company of the Nasdaq purchased the Amex, although the two continue to operate separately. Orders for stock are sent out electronically on the Nasdaq, where market makers list their buy and sell prices. Once a price is agreed upon, the transaction is executed electronically.

Net Asset Value (NAV)

NAV equals the closing market value of all assets within a portfolio after subtracting all liabilities including accrued fees and expenses. NAV per share is the NAV divided by the number of shares in issue. This is often used as the price of a fund. A purchase fee may be added to the NAV when buying units in the fund. This fee is typically 1-7%.

Net Exposure

The exposure level of a fund to the market. It is calculated by subtracting the short percentage from the long percentage. For example if a fund is 100% long and 30% short, then the net exposure is 70% long.

Nominee Name

Name in which a security is registered and held in trust on behalf of the beneficial owner.

O

Offer Price

The price at which a fund manager or market maker will sell shares to you. (ie offer them to you). The offer price is higher than the Bid Price which is the price at which they will buy shares from you. (ie they will make a bid). This is one way in which a market maker turns a profit. A fund manager may use the difference to cover dealing administration costs.

Offshore

Located or based outside of one's national boundaries. Typically these locations have preferential tax treatments and fund legislation.

Open Architecture

In relation to funds, for example FPIL Reserve policyholders may choose any security – open architecture. In contrast to FPIL Premier policyholders who may only go into the FPIL mirror fund range – this is guided architecture.

Open-ended Funds

These are funds where units or shares can be bought and sold daily and where the number of units or shares in issue can vary daily.

Opportunistic Investing

A general term describing any fund that is opportunistic in nature. These types of funds are usually aggressive and seek to make money in the most efficient way at any given time. Investment themes are dominated by events that are seen as special situations or short-term opportunities to capitalise from price fluctuations or imbalances, such as initial public offering.

Option

A privilege sold by one party to another that offers the buyer the right, but not the obligation, to buy (call)or sell (put) a security at an agreed-upon price during a certain period of time or on a specific date. Options are extremely versatile securities that can be used in many different ways. Traders use optionsto speculate, which is a relatively risky practice, while hedgers use options to reduce the risk of holding an asset.

Over the Counter- OTC

A security traded in some context other than on a formal exchange such as the LSE, NYSE, DJIA, TSX, AMEX, etc. A stock is traded over the counter usually because the company is small and unable to meet listing requirements of the exchanges. Also known as unlisted stock, these securities are traded by brokers/dealers who negotiate directly with one another over computer networks and by phone. The Nasdaq, however, is also considered to be an OTC market, with the tier 1 being represented bycompanies such as Microsoft, Dell and Intel. Instruments such as bonds do not trade on a formal exchange and are thus considered over-the- counter securities. Most debt instruments are traded byinvestment banks making markets for specific issues. If someone wants to buy or sell a bond, they callthe bank that makes the market in that bond and ask for quotes. Many derivative instruments such as forwards, swaps and most exotic derivatives are also traded OTC.

Out of the Money

This refers to options :

1) For a call, when an option's strike price is higher than the market price of the underlying stock.

2) For a put, when the strike price is below the market price of the underlying stock.

Basically, an option that would be worthless if it expired today.

Over-Hedging

Locking in a price, such as through a futures contract, for more goods, commodities or securities that is required to protect a position. While hedging does protect a position, over-hedging can be costly in the form of missed opportunities. Although you can lock in a selling price, over-hedging might result in a producer or seller missing out on favourable market prices. For example, if you entered into a January futures contract to sell 25,000 shares of 'Smith Holdings' at $6.50 per share you would not be able to take advantage if the spot price jumped to $7.00.

Overlay Strategy

A type of derivatives strategy. This strategy is often employed to provide protection from currencies or interest rate movements that are not the primary focus of the main portfolio strategy.

Overweight

Refers to an investment position that is larger than the generally accepted benchmark. For example, if a company normally holds a portfolio whose weighting of cash is 10%, and then increases cash holdings to 15%, the portfolio would have an overweight position in cash.

P

Pair Trading

The strategy of matching a long position with a short position in two stocks of the same sector. This creates a hedge against the sector and the overall market that the two stocks are in. The hedge createdis essentially a bet that you are placing on the two stocks; the stock you are long in versus the stock you are short in. It's the ultimate strategy for stock pickers, because stock picking is all that counts. What the actual market does won't matter (much). If the market or the sector moves in one direction or the other, the gain on the long stock is offset by a loss on the short.

Percent Long

The percentage of a fund invested in long positions.

Percent Short

The percentage of a fund that is sold short.

Performance Fee

The fee payable to the fund adviser on new profits earned by the fund for the period.

Portfolio Turnover

The number of times an average portfolio security is replaced during an accounting period, usually a year.

Premium

The total cost of an option. The premium of an option is basically the sum of the option's intrinsic and time value. It is important to note that volatility also affects the premium.

The difference between the higher price paid for a fixed-income security and the security's face amount at issue. If a fixed-income security (bond) is purchased at a premium, existing interest rates are lower than the coupon rate. Investors pay a premium for an investment that will return an amount greater than existing interest rates.

Price Earnings Ratio (P/E Ratio)

A valuation ratio of a company's current share price compared to its per-share earnings. Calculated as: Market Value per Share/Earnings per Share (EPS)

EPS is usually from the last four quarters (trailing P/E), but sometimes can be taken from the estimates of earnings expected in the next four quarters (projected or forward P/E). A third variation is the sum of the last two actual quarters and the estimates of the next two quarters.

Sometimes the P/E is referred to as the "multiple," because it shows how much investors are willing to pay per dollar of earnings. In general, a high P/E means high projected earnings in the future. However, the P/E ratio actually doesn't tell us a whole lot by itself. It's usually only useful to compare the P/E ratios of companies in the same industry, or to the market in general, or against the company's own historical P/E.

Prime Broker

A broker which acts as settlement agent, provides custody for assets, provides financing for leverage, and prepares daily account statements for its clients, who might be money managers, hedge funds, market makers, arbitrageurs, specialists and other professional investors.

Private Placement / Private Equity

When equity capital is made available to companies or investors, but not quoted on a stock market. The funds raised through private equity can be used to develop new products and technologies, to expand working capital, to make acquisitions, or to strengthen a company's balance sheet. The average individual investor will not have access to private equity because it requires a very large investment. The result is the sale of securities to a relatively small number of investors.

Private placements do not have to be registered with organizations such as the FSA, SEC because no public offering is involved.

Proprietary Trading

When a firm trades for direct gain instead of commission dollars. Essentially, the firm has decided to profit from the market rather than commissions from processing trades. Firms who engage in proprietary trading believe they have a competitive advantage that will enable them to earn excess returns.

Prospectus

In the case of mutual funds, a prospectus describes the fund's objectives, history, manager background, and financial statements. A prospectus makes investors aware of the risks of an investment and in most jurisdictions is required to be published by law.

Protected Cell Company

A standard limited company that has been separated into legally distinct portions or cells. The revenue streams, assets and liabilities of each cell are kept separate from all other cells. Each cell has its own separate portion of the PCC's overall share capital, allowing shareholders to maintain sole ownership of an entire cell while owning only a small proportion of the PCC as a whole. PCCs can provide a means of entry into a captive insurance market to entities for which it was previously uneconomic. The overheads of a protected cell captive can be shared between the owners of each of the cells, making the captive cheaper to run from the point of view of the insured.

Purification

The process whereby Muslims give to charity any interest deemed to have been credited to their holdings in funds or stocks.

Put Option

An option giving the holder the right, but not the obligation, to sell a specific quantity of an asset for a fixed price during a specific period.

Q

Qualitative Analysis
Analysis that uses subjective judgment in evaluating securities based on non-financial information such as management expertise, cyclicality of industry, strength of research and development, and labour relations.

Quantitative Analysis
A security analysis that uses financial information derived from company annual reports and income statements to evaluate an investment decision. Some examples are financial ratios, the cost of capital, asset valuation, and sales and earnings trends.

Quasi Sovereign Bond
Debt issued by a public sector entity that is, like a sovereign bond, guaranteed by the sovereign, however there is a difference in that there may be a timing difference in repayment in the unlikely event of default.

R

REIT Real Estate Investment Trust
A security that trades like a stock on the major exchanges and invests in real estate directly, through either properties or mortgages.

REITs receive special tax considerations and typically offer investors high yields, as well as a highly liquid method of investing in real estate. Equity REITs invest in and own properties (thus responsible for the equity or value of their real estate assets). Their revenues come principally from their properties' rents. Mortgage REITs deal in investment and ownership of property mortgages. These REITs loan money for mortgages to owners of real estate, or purchase existing mortgages or mortgage-backed securities. Their revenues are generated primarily by the interest that they earn on the mortgage loans. Hybrid REITs combine the investment strategies of equity REITs and mortgage REITs by investing in both properties and mortgages.

R – Squared

A statistical measure that represents the percentage of a fund's or security's movements that are explained by movements in a benchmark index. It is a measure of correlation with the benchmark.R-squared values range from 0 to 100. An R-squared of 100 means that all movements of a security are completely explained by movements in the index. ie perfect correlation.

Repurchase Agreement (Repo)

A form of short-term borrowing for dealers in government securities. The dealer sells the government securities to investors, usually on an overnight basis, and buys them back the following day. For the party selling the security (and agreeing to repurchase it in the future) it is a repo; for the party on the other end of the transaction (buying the security and agreeing to sell in the future) it is a reverse repurchase agreement. Repos are classified as a money-market instrument. They are usually used toraise short-term capital.

Risk Adjusted Rate of Return

A measure of how much risk a fund or portfolio took on to earn its returns, usually expressed as a number or a rating. This is often represented by the Sharpe Ratio. The more return per unit of risk, the better

Risk Arbitrage

A broad definition for three types of arbitrage that contain an element of risk:

1) Merger and Acquisition Arbitrage - The simultaneous purchase of stock in a company being acquired and the sale (or short sale) of stock in the acquiring company.

2) Liquidation Arbitrage - The exploitation of a difference between a company's current value and its estimated liquidation value.

3) Pairs Trading - The exploitation of a difference between two very similar companies in the same industry that have historically been highly correlated. When the two company's values diverge to a historically high level you can take an offsetting position in each (e.g. go long in one and short the other) because, as history has shown, they will inevitably come to be similarly valued.

In theory true arbitrage is riskless, however, the world in which we operate offers very few of these opportunities. Despite these forms of arbitrage being somewhat risky, they are still relatively low-risk trading strategies which money managers (mainly hedge fund managers) and retail investors alike can employ.

Risk-Free Rate

The quoted rate on an asset that has virtually no risk. The rate quoted for US treasury bills are widely used as the risk free rate.

Risk Reward Ratio

This is closely related to the Sharpe Ratio, except the risk reward ratio does not use a risk free rate in its calculation. The higher the risk reward ratio, the better. Calculated as : Annualised rate of return/Annualised Standard Deviation

S

Santa Claus Rally

The rise in US stock prices that sometimes occurs in the week after Christmas, often in anticipation of the January effect.

Satellite Fund

Specialist mandate fund that offers greater breadth of proposition than a "core" fund.

Secondary Market

A market in which an investor purchases an asset from another investor, rather than an issuing corporation. A good example is the London Stock Exchange. All stock exchanges are part of the secondary market, as investors buy securities from other investors instead of an issuing company.

Sector Fund

A mutual fund whose objective is to invest in a particular industry or sector of the economy to capitalizeon returns. Because most of the stocks in this type of fund are all in the same industry, there is a lack ofdiversification. The fund tends to do very well or not well at all, depending on the conditions of the specific sector.

Securities

General name for all stocks and shares of all types.

Securities Lending

When a brokerage lends securities owned by its clients to short sellers. This allows brokers to create additional revenue (commissions) on the short sale transaction.

Semi-gilt

A financial instrument through which a municipality or parastatal (owned or controlled wholly or partly by the government) borrows money from the public in exchange for a fixed repayment plan.

SICAV

SICAV stands for Societe D'Investissement a Capital Variable. It is a Luxembourg incorporated company that is responsible for the management of a mutual fund and manages a portfolio of securities. The share capital is equal to the net assets of the fund. The units in the portfolio are delivered as shares and the investors are referred to as shareholders. SICAVs are common fund structures in Luxembourg.

Sharia(h)

Sharia refers to the body of Islamic law. The term means "way" or "path"; it is the legal framework within which public and some private aspects of life are regulated for those living in a legal system based on Muslim principles.

Sharpe Ratio
A ratio developed by Bill Sharpe to measure risk-adjusted performance. It is calculated by subtracting the risk free rate from the rate of return for a portfolio and dividing the result by the standard deviation of the portfolio returns.

Calculated as: Expected Portfolio Return − Risk Free Rate/Portfolio Standard Deviation

The Sharpe ratio tells us whether the returns of a portfolio are because of smart investment decisions or a result of excess risk. The Sortino Ratio is a variation of this.

Short Selling
The selling of a security that the seller does not own, or any sale that is completed by the delivery of a security borrowed by the seller. Short sellers assume that they will be able to buy the stock at a lower amount than the price at which they sold short. Selling short is the opposite of going long. That is, short sellers make money if the stock goes down in price. This is an advanced trading strategy with many unique risks and pitfalls.

Small Caps
Stocks or funds with smaller capitalisation. They tend to be less liquid than blue chips, but they tend to have higher returns.

Soft Commissions
A means of paying brokerage firms for their services through commission revenue, as opposed to normal payments. For example, a mutual fund may offer to pay for the research of a brokerage firm by executing trades at the brokerage.

Sovereign Debt
A debt instrument guaranteed by a government.
Special Situations Investing
Strategy that seeks to profit from pricing discrepancies resulting from corporate event transactions such as mergers

and acquisitions, spin-offs, bankruptcies or recapitalisations. Type of event-driven strategy.

Specific Risk

Risk that affects a very small number of assets. This is sometimes referred to as "unsystematic risk." An example would be news that is specific to either one stock or a small number of stocks, such as a sudden strike by the employees of a company you have shares in or a new governmental regulation affecting a particular group of companies. Unlike systematic risk or market risk, specific risk can be diversified away.

Spin Off

A new, independent company created through selling or distributing new shares for an existing part of another company. Spinoffs may be done through a rights offering.

Sponsors

Lead investors in a fund who supply the seed money. Often the general partner in a hedge fund.

Spread

1) The difference between the bid and the offer prices of a security or asset.

2) An options position established by purchasing one option and selling another option of the same class, but of a different series

Standard Deviation

Tells us how much the return on the fund is deviating from the expected normal returns.

Stop-Loss Order

An order placed with a broker to sell a security when it reaches a certain price. It is designed to limit an investor's loss on a security position. This is sometimes called a "stop market order." In other words, setting a stop-loss order for 10% below the price you paid for the stock would limit your loss to 10%.

Strategic Bond Funds

Invest primarily in higher yielding assets including high yield bonds, investment grade bonds, preference shares and other bonds. The funds take strategic asset allocation decisions between countries, asset classes, sectors and credit ratings.

Strike Price

The stated price per share for which underlying stock may be purchased (for a call) or sold (for a put) by the option holder upon exercise of the option contract.

Swap

Traditionally, the exchange of one security for another to change the maturity (bonds), quality of issues (stocks or bonds), or because investment objectives have changed. Recently, swaps have grown to include currency swaps and interest rates swaps. If firms in separate countries have comparative advantages on interest rates, then a swap could benefit both firms. For example, one firm may have a lower fixed interest rate, while another has access to a lower floating interest rate. These firms could swap to take advantage of the lower rates.

Swaption (Swap Option)

The option to enter into an interest rate swap. In exchange for an option premium, the buyer gains the right but not the obligation to enter into a specified swap agreement with the issuer on a specified future date.

Swing Trading (Swings)

A style of trading that attempts to capture gains in a stock within one to four days. To find situations in which a stock has this extraordinary potential to move in such a short time frame, the trader must act quickly. This is mainly used by at-home and day traders. Large institutions trade in sizes too big to move in and out of stocks quickly. The individual trader is able to exploit the short-term stock movements without the competition of major traders. Swing traders use technical analysis to look for stocks with short-term price momentum. These traders aren't interested in the fundamental or intrinsic value of stocks but rather in their price trends and patterns.

Systematic Risk

The risk inherent to the entire market or entire market segment. Also known as "un-diversifiable risk" or "market risk." interest rates, recession and wars all represent sources of systematic risk because they will affect the entire market and cannot be avoided through diversification. Whereas this type of risk affects a broad range of securities, unsystematic risk affects a very specific group of securities or an individual security. Systematic risk can be mitigated only by being hedged.

Systemic Risk

Risk that threatens an entire financial system.

S&P500

Standard & Poor's Index of the New York Stock Exchange. A basket of 500 stocks that are considered to be widely held. The S&P 500 index is weighted by market value, and its performance is thought to be representative of the stock market as a whole.

T

Treasury Bill

A negotiable debt obligation issued by the U.S. government and backed by its full faith and credit, having a maturity of one year or less. Exempt from state and local taxes. Also called Bill or T-Bill or U.S. Treasury Bill.

Time Value

The amount by which an option's premium exceeds its intrinsic value. Also called time premium.

Top-Down Investing

An investment strategy which first finds the best sectors or industries to invest in, and then searches for the best companies within those sectors or industries. This investing strategy begins with a look at the overall economic picture and then narrows it down to sectors, industries and companies that are expected to perform well. Analysis of the fundamentals of a given security is the final step.

Tracking Error

This statistic measures the standard deviation of a fund's excess returns over the returns of an index or benchmark portfolio. As such, it can be an indication of 'riskiness' in the manager's investment style. A Tracking Error below 2 suggests a passive approach, with a close fit between the fund and its benchmark. At 3 and above the correlation is progressively looser: the manager will be deploying a more active investment style, and taking bigger positions away from the benchmark's composition.

Traded Endowment Policy - TEP

An Endowment Policy is a type of life insurance that has a value that is payable to the insured if he/she is still living on the policy's maturity date, or to a beneficiary otherwise. They are normally "with profits policies". If the insured does not wish to wait until maturity to receive the value they can either surrender it back to the issuing insurance company, or they can sell the policy on the open market. If the policy is sold it then becomes a Traded Endowment Policy or TEP. TEP Funds aim to buy and sell TEPs at advantageous prices to make a profit.

Traded Options

Transferable options with the right to buy or sell a standardised amount of a security at a fixed price within a specified period.

Traditional Investments

Includes equities, bonds, high yield bonds, emerging markets debt, cash, cash equivalents.

U

Umbrella Fund

An investment company which has a group of sub-funds (pools) each having its own investment portfolio. The purpose of this structure is to provide investment flexibility and widen investor choice.

Underlier or Underlying Security

A security or commodity, which is subject to delivery upon exercise of an option contract or convertible security. Exceptions include index options and futures, which cannot be delivered and are therefore settled in cash.

Underweight

A situation where a portfolio does not hold a sufficient amount of securities to satisfy the accepted benchmark of the portfolio's asset allocation strategy. For example, if a portfolio normally holds 40% stock and currently holds 30%, the position in equities would be considered underweight.

Unit Trust

A common form of collective investment (similar to a mutual fund) where investors' money is pooled and invested into a variety of shares and bonds in order to reduce risk. Its capital structure is open ended as units can be created or redeemed depending on demand from investors. It should be noted that a Unit Trust means something completely different in the US.

V

Value of New Business VNB

Sum of all income (i.e. charges) from new policies minus costs of setting up the policies (i.e. commission) discounted to present day value.

Value Stocks

Stocks which are perceived to be selling at a discount to their intrinsic or potential worth, i.e. undervalued; or stocks which are out of favour with the market and are under-followed by analysts. It is believed that the share price of these stocks will increase as the value of the company is recognised by the market.

Value-Added Monthly Index (VAMI)
An index that tracks the monthly performance of a hypothetical $1000 investment. The calculation for the current month's VAMI is: Previous VAMI x (1 + Current Rate of Return)

The value-added monthly index charts the total return gained by an investor from reinvestment of any dividends and additional interest gained through compounding. The VAMI index is sometimes used to evaluate the performance of a fund manager.

Venture Capital
Money and resources made available to start-up firms and small businesses with exceptional growth potential. Venture capital often also includes managerial and technical expertise. Most venture capital money comes from an organized group of wealthy investors who seek substantially above average returns and who are willing to accept correspondingly high risks. This form of raising capital is increasingly popular among new companies that, because of a limited operating history, can't raise money through a debt issue. The downside for entrepreneurs is that venture capitalists usually receive a say in the major decisions of the company in addition to a portion of the equity.

Volatility
Standard deviation is a statistical measurement which, when applied to an investment fund, expresses its volatility, or risk. It shows how widely a range of returns varied from the fund's average return over a particular period. Low volatility reduces the risk of buying into an investment in the upper range of its deviation cycle, then seeing its value head towards the lower extreme. For example, if a fund had an average return of 5%, and its volatility was 15, this would mean that the range of its returns over the period had swung between +20% and -10%.

Another fund with the same average return and 5% volatility would return between 10% and nothing, but there would at least be no loss.

Made in the USA
Charleston, SC
16 January 2017